Confessions of a SCREAM QUEEN

by **MATT BECKOFF**

CONFESSIONS OF A SCREAM QUEEN
©2010 MATT BECKOFF

Published in the USA by:

BEARMANOR MEDIA
P.O. BOX 71426
ALBANY, GEORGIA 31708
www.BearManorMedia.com

All photos are from the Author's collection, except where noted.
Marilyn Burns photos courtesy of Marilyn Burns.
Dee Wallace photos courtesy of Dee Wallace.
P.J. Soles photos courtesy of P.J. Soles.
Judith O'Dea photos courtesy of Judith O'Dea.
Ingrid Pitt photos courtesy of Ingrid Pitt.
Coleen Gray photos courtesy of Coleen Gray.
Kathleen Hughes photos courtesy of Kathleen Hughes.

ISBN-10: 1-59393-539-0 (alk. paper)
ISBN-13: 973-1-59393-539-9 (alk. paper)

Printed in the United States of America.

COPY EDITORS: DAVID W. MENEFEE AND DR. JEFF THOMPSON

COVER DESIGN: RAY A. SEDA

BOOK DESIGN AND LAYOUT: VALERIE THOMPSON

Table of Contents

Acknowledgments

I want to thank the following people for helping me along the way with this book. In no particular order: Ray Seda, Pancho Kohner, Victoria Alpert Elbrecht, Ben Ohmart, Martin Grams, Gordon Reid, Dennis Brookins, Andrew Sigman, Rob Aragon, Elizabeth McLaughlin, Dr. Jeff Thompson, and Larry Storch.

Very special thanks to my good friend Rick Atkins for all his help and inspiration. Thanks to my friends and family for all their support.

This book is dedicated to all horror fans and the fifteen incredible actresses who were kind enough to be included in this book. I cannot thank you all enough.

Foreword

There have been many books written about movie stars. Being an old "Monster Kid" myself, I have most all of the books on horror and science fiction films, but my friend Matt has written one that I feel is different than most. His book is from the 1930s to the 1980s on the "Ladies of Horror." In *Confessions of a Scream Queen*, some of the ladies he has interviewed are Carla Laemmle, Elena Verdugo, Lupita Tovar, Coleen Gray, Ingrid Pitt, plus many more. The difference in this book is that Matt also delves into the ladies' beginnings, and it is fascinating reading. One learns a lot about early Hollywood, as well. The interview with Ingrid Pitt is a hoot. She is a free spirit. I think that other "Monster Kids" and movie buffs as well will like this book. I'd sure want it in my collection. Matt gets a big two KONG size thumbs up on a great book!

BOB BURNS 2010

Author's Note

What exactly is a "Scream Queen?" It would seem irrelevant to try and define the commonly used term. There have been many books, television specials, and documentaries on the subject over the years. According to an online information source, a "Scream Queen" is defined as follows: an actress who became associated with horror films, either through an appearance in a notable entry in the genre as a frequent victim, or through constant appearances as the female protagonist. Sounds pretty good to me.

So why did I go about putting this book together? Rather than the normal 2,500-word or less interview in a magazine or column, I decided to give these women free range. I didn't want snippets. I wanted everything they wanted to share, and I was more than happy to listen.

Over the years, "Scream Queens" have taken many shapes, sizes, and screams! Included in this book are fifteen conversations with these respected ladies of the silver screen. Some of these ladies have danced at the Paris Opera House where the Phantom crept, been chased after by a rabid dog, tortured by a tiny doll with a knife, pounced on by the hairy Wolf Man, and attacked by a chainsaw-wielding psychopath. Fortunately for us, they lived to tell about it.

Chapter One:
CARLA LAEMMLE

At ninety-nine years of age, one would think a person begins to slow down. This is not so with Carla Laemmle; she is busier than ever. The year 2009 saw the release of two books from Ms. Laemmle, the first of which is a biography titled *Among the Rugged Peaks: An Intimate Biography of Carla Laemmle*, published by Midnight Marquee Press, which gets its namesake from her opening lines in the original 1931 classic motion picture, *Dracula* made at Universal Pictures. (Carla is the last surviving cast member.)

A second book was published by BearManor Media entitled, *Growing up with Monsters: My Times At Universal Studios in Rhymes!* It is a book about Carla's years living on the Universal lot. She is the niece of Universal founder Carl Laemmle.

I had the pleasure of interviewing Carla a few hours prior to her first book signing that was held in Burbank, California. The following day, she was scheduled to appear at another signing in Los Angeles. With fame coming to Carla later in life, she shows no signs of slowing down and loves every minute of it.

MATT: You were originally a dancer, correct?

CARLA: Yes. I started dancing when I was six years old. My mother thought it was amusing, when I was a baby, I kept wiggling my toes all the time, and for some weird reason, my mother thought that it indicated I wanted to be a dancer. How she ever figured that? But, I did want to be a dancer.

A rare photo of Carla dancing in the 1920s.

And whenever any music was played, I would get up and dance. My mother soon gave me dancing lessons. We moved out here to Hollywood, and I studied under Ernest Belcher, who was later hired as the choreographer for *The Phantom of the Opera* with Lon Chaney.

MATT: Do you think it was Mr. Belcher who helped you get cast in the movie?

CARLA: Yes, I think that he felt that my uncle would be pleased to have his niece be a ballerina, and since I was up to it, they cast me as Prima Ballerina.

MATT: Can you tell me how you got your start in show business?

CARLA: Well, when I was eleven years old, my family moved out to California from Chicago, and we lived right on the Universal lot. I was a dancer from the very beginning and I kept taking dancing lessons. By the time I was sixteen, I was premier ballerina in *The Phantom of the Opera* with Lon Chaney.

MATT: What was the experience like appearing in the 1925 version of *The Phantom of The Opera*?

CARLA: Oh, it was fantastic! The stage itself was a replica of the original and it was enormous! And they had a chorus line of girls dancing behind me. I was doing what they call a "Pas de deux," that is with a partner, and we do a lot of lifts and things like that. I have photos of that someplace (laughs). So, that was when I was just sixteen.

MATT: Did you get to know Lon Chaney at all?

CARLA: No, I never met him. We were in no scenes together.

MATT: So, you never saw him transform from Lon Chaney into the Phantom?

CARLA: No, but as I understand he was a master of makeup, and he did his own makeup. It took, I think, over two hours for him to make himself up as the Phantom. However, earlier at Universal, I did watch some scenes being filmed of him as *The Hunchback of Notre Dame*. His body had to be padded and hunched back. He had these, I don't know, they looked like walnuts inside his cheeks, to bring them out. It was terrifying, yet it was sad, you know, because he wasn't an evil character. It was wonderful in this one particular scene. He was climbing down from the cathedral and he did it all himself. He had no doubles, he did everything himself and it was pretty remarkable being able to watch that.

MATT: Weren't you close friends with Mary Philbin, who played Christine Daae?

CARLA: (Smiles) Yes, we knew one another well. We were neighbors as a matter of fact in Chicago. She was six years older than I, but still we were just very good friends. We loved one another a lot.

MATT: I read somewhere that you took care of Mary Philbin in her later years when she was ill.

CARLA: I did? Wherever you read that it was a mistake. I don't know where she spent her days when she got a little older. That's just a rumor.

MATT: Glad we cleared that up then. Your uncle, Carl Laemmle, was the founder of Universal Studios. Can you tell me a little about him personally?

CARLA: He was just wonderful, and he was very intelligent. You can imagine coming over here from Germany as a young eighteen-year-old, whatever it was, a young age with $50 in his pocket. He had previously worked with a family member who knew English, and it was through him that he was able to learn enough English to get by. And then, of course, when he got here, he naturally began to learn more English by continually talking with people. And he managed it beautifully, because, when I knew him he spoke great English. Of course there was his familiar German accent! But outside of that he commanded the language, just amazing! He was a very smart individual.

MATT: How did Carl Laemmle feel about the Universal horror pictures?

CARLA: Carl Laemmle wasn't too fond of the horror movies. However, his son Carl Laemmle, Jr., was hooked on them. He convinced his father that they should go into it and it was certainly a wise idea. Imagine my uncle today, and "Junior" to know, that *Dracula*, over seventy years later is still a classic.

MATT: Over seventy-five years!

CARLA: Over seventy-five years, there you go! I had spoken the first lines of dialogue. I'm sort of a cult figure, which I find amusing.

MATT: *Dracula* was the first "talkie" horror film. Is that true?

CARLA: It was.

MATT: So, you ushered in the first line of any horror film!

CARLA: Actually, I never thought of it, that way, but it's true (laughs)!

MATT: What was it like filming your scene in *Dracula*?

A still from _Dracula_ 1931 featuring Carla Laemmle.

CARLA: It was fun and interesting. There were several people in the coach scene, like Dwight Frye, who was one of them. It was filmed on the back lot at Universal Studios. There were several so-called property men, who were standing outside the coach. You couldn't see them in camera range, but they would keep jiggling the coach back and forth to give the illusion it was moving. And so, that was how those scenes were done.

MATT: Did you spend any time with Bela Lugosi on set?

CARLA: No, I never met him.

MATT: Was it true that Lon Chaney was originally hired for the role of Dracula?

CARLA: I think he was considered, but that sort of went down the drain.

MATT: Do you have any particular favorite memories of *Dracula*?

CARLA: It was so much fun doing the scene in the coach, and being scared, you know, the jiggling of the coach and I had to fall over Dwight Frye's lap. It was only a day to do the whole sequence, it wasn't any big thing, but, it was something that you don't forget, you know.

MATT: I can imagine. It's funny how just one day of your life has such an impact all these years later. A lot of people around the world love you just from that one day of your ninety-nine years.

CARLA: Isn't that something (laughs)?

MATT: After all these years, does it amaze you that such a relatively small part has gotten you such attention?

CARLA: Oh yes, it's fabulous. Well, it never entered my thoughts that it was going to turn out to be a classic horror movie, you know. I couldn't have dreamed of anything like that.

MATT: Well, both *The Phantom of the Opera* and *Dracula* are classics! And you are the only cast member from either film from what I believe. Correct?

CARLA: I believe so.

MATT: We touched on this before, but I want to hear more about it. What was it like growing up on the lot at Universal when so much was happening?

CARLA: It was fabulous! I loved every minute of it, every year of it! I was there sixteen years. My "Uncle Carl" sold the studio in 1936. We moved from there in 1937.

MATT: You must have seen a lot of great productions of other movies being filmed, considering it was your back yard.

CARLA: Well, where we lived was right off of Lankershim Boulevard. It was right by the entrance to the studio, and of course, the main studios with the stages were a bit away from where we lived. But right in back of our house was New York Street, and that was a duplicate of New York City. I used to enjoy going over there and just walking around and imagining I was really there in New York City. It was just great fun, especially for a young person coming from Chicago. It was a fantasy world to live in!

MATT: How did it feel moving off the lot?

CARLA: We moved to a bungalow. It was all right, but it wasn't Universal Studios. I missed that so much.

MATT: Have you been back to Universal since?

CARLA: They took our home down! Other things were put there. The whole Universal lot is completely different from the time when I lived there. See, when we moved there, Universal was only six years old; it was new. They were more or less creating it when I was there. My uncle had the lot built at Universal City just for moviemaking, but it was supposed to be like a little city, which it was. It was incorporated. It had everything that a city has. It had a hospital, fire department, even a mayor—a woman mayor, as a matter of fact—everything a city has. It was enchanting growing up there.

MATT: Though most people know you from *The Phantom of the Opera* and *Dracula*, you also did other movies. You worked with Frank Sinatra.

CARLA: Yes, I did. I have some photos.

MATT: *Step Lively?*

CARLA: Yes, *Step Lively*. You knew it!

MATT: What was it like working with Frank Sinatra?

CARLA: I was enchanted by his voice. He had such great talent. He was very young then.

MATT: You were also in a movie called *The Broadway Melody*. However, your scene was filmed previously for a different movie, but ended up in *The Broadway Melody*?

CARLA: Yes, that's correct. It's confusing, because I associated it with the other movie for a while. In my scene, I came out of an oyster shell that came up out of the floor somehow. And then it opened up, and there I was, in the oyster. I got out and I did this seductive dance, and then I went back into the oyster shell and disappeared. That was for MGM and not Universal. They borrowed me for some reason. I don't know why (laughs)?

MATT: You were in a very long relationship with actor/writer/director Raymond Cannon. Can you share some of that with me?

CARLA: He was the most important person in my life. I

met him in 1935 at Universal, when he was a director. I was cast in one of his little comedy shorts that he was directing, and that's how I met him. He was interested in the Eastern philosophy, Zen and Taoism. I was also interested in the Eastern philosophy, so we had that in common. I fell in love with him right away.

MATT: I read in your book, *Among the Rugged Peaks*, that Raymond wrote a play for you?

CARLA: He did. It was called *Her Majesty the Prince*. It was a Chinese play. I had only known him a year, when he started writing the play for me. It was produced at the Music Box Theatre in Hollywood, in 1936. That was the most fabulous experience that I could remember.

MATT: That's your favorite experience from your whole career?

CARLA: Yes, absolutely. It was such a delightful play. The whole thing was all of these Chinese characters. I had an opportunity to do a Chinese dance. It was just an utterly enchanting play. We were all made up to be Chinese.

MATT: In 2001, you revisited the Stage 28 set, *The Phantom of the Opera* stage on the Universal lot. After seventy years, what was it like being there again?

CARLA: It was a wonderful trip! It was thrilling being back there. I loved being there once again, were I appeared in the ballet. It was a great experience.

MATT: Did it look very different from what you remember?

Carla on the legendary *Phantom of the Opera* soundstage in 2009.
PHOTO COURTESY OF TOM TANGEN.

CARLA: Oh yes, it's all very different, except stage 28; that's almost like a sacred place. They won't change that. It will be there forever, unless an earthquake comes and breaks it down (laughs).

MATT: You published a biography recently. Can you tell me about the book?

CARLA: My good friend, Rick Atkins, wrote it. He had previously written a book about movie people. We traveled to Germany together. I have some very wonderful friends and family there, one of whom is Udo Bayer. He has been working on Carl Laemmle's biography for many years. He got in touch with me, and so I visited him in Germany. On one occasion, Rick went with me to Germany in 1999. Udo, who knew Rick was a writer, asked Rick, "Why don't you consider writing Carla's biography?" So, he asked me one day, if I would consider it, if I'd be interested, and I said, "Why not?" So, that's how that happened. It's a "tell all" book. I decided I wouldn't soften anything. I decided I wouldn't cheat on anything. I told it like it was. If my uncle and family were alive, then maybe I wouldn't have done the book the way I did. They would not approve of it, you know, certain things that I reveal in the book.

MATT: The photos in the book are great. There are even some rather racy photos of you from way back when.

CARLA: Yes! That should sell the book, just by itself (laughs)!

MATT: Did you enjoy looking back on your career for the biography?

Carla with Ray Bradbury at her 100th Birthday celebration in 2009.
PHOTO BY MATT BECKOFF.

CARLA: Of course, I did! It's fantastic to me, at ninety-nine, to have this sudden interest in my life. I never felt myself to be a celebrity. Now, everyone thinks I'm a real celebrity. I guess I'm one from the past, one of the few people that has survived to this point.

MATT: Are there any secrets to longevity?

CARLA: No, not that I know of. I don't drink, and I don't smoke. You know there is a little Chinese saying that I live by: "Harm no one, especially yourself!" Those are some pretty powerful words. And I try to live by that. I think a positive frame of mind is important.

MATT: Carla, thank you so much for a wonderful interview.

CARLA: It was fun! Thank you!

MATT: One last thing Carla. Could you recite your infamous opening line for me?

CARLA: Oh, Yes. Sure! (Clears her throat) "Among the rugged peaks that frown down upon the Borgo Pass are found crumbling castles of the bygone age."

MATT: Wonderful! Thank you so much!

CARLA: You're very welcome.

Chapter Two:
LUPITA TOVAR

Life is full of great debates, such as which came first, the chicken or the egg? Is it Nature or Nurture? For many classic horror movie buffs, it comes down to which *Dracula* 1931 version was better: the English version, or the Spanish version? It's not an easy question to answer. How can they be that different to begin with? They were filmed on the same sets, they were produced by the same studio, and the Spanish cast was told to duplicate what the American cast did. And yet, the films are different, with some saying that one is better than the other.

Lupita Tovar is one person of whom you don't need to ask the question. When she says which version is better, you believe it! She is confident the Spanish version is superior. She appeared as the Mina character, named "Eva" in the Spanish version of *Dracula*. Lupita also appeared in many other films. She is best known to Mexican audiences for the classic film, *Santa*. In 2009, I had the great honor of speaking to the legendary Mexican actress over the telephone just a few weeks shy of her ninety-ninth birthday.

MATT: You got your start by being discovered in Mexico City. Can you tell me about that?

LUPITA: Mr. Robert Flaherty discovered me. He was a director from Fox Studios. He went to Mexico City looking for new talent. He came along with an assistant to visit my school where they saw me doing gymnastics in my black bloomers and tennis shoes. That was the first time they looked at me.

MATT: What happened next?

LUPITA: About ten days later I was in a contest organized by the leading newspaper in Mexico City, *El Universal,* and I won first prize. I had no idea. Little did they know that I came to this country in 1928 accompanied by my grandmother, Miss Lucy Sullivan, who was my mother's mother. Fox studio brought me over, and then unfortunately the talkies came. I spoke no English. It was very poor. I was let go by Fox studios, but I didn't want to go back to Mexico a failure. Soon, they started dubbing films in different languages at Universal. So, I started dubbing there for $15.00 a night.

MATT: Back then, that was a lot of money.

LUPITA: Goodness it was a lot of money. We worked from seven in the evening until seven in the morning.

MATT: That sounds like a hard schedule to keep.

LUPITA: Well, I'll tell you something, Matt. I was determined not to go back to Mexico as a failure. I had to do something. I couldn't just go back! When my contract at Fox ended, I was worried because of the talkies. Every penny I was making I sent to my father so they could buy a home in Mexico. I had no money here. But I didn't want to go back to doing nothing.

I came into this world with Halley's Comet. When my mother was giving birth, she said she could see through her window the tail of the comet Halley. That's when I was born. If you believe in astrology, it means something *especial.*

MATT: What was the studio system like during the transition from silent films to talkies?

LUPITA: It was chaos, especially for the people in the silent films. Big stars were out of jobs. Big, big stars like Ramon Novarro. They started bringing people from the New York stage for the talkies because they were the only ones that knew how to talk. They were very stagy. It took me a while to adjust and for me to be natural.

MATT: So, Universal had started to make foreign language films. What were some early Spanish films you appeared in?

LUPITA: The first was *La voluntad del muerto (The Cat and the Canary)*.

MATT: The Spanish version of *The Cat Creeps*?

LUPITA: Yes, *The Cat Creeps*. (A lost film.)

MATT: What was it like being so young and new to Hollywood and already starring in a film?

LUPITA: Well, I'll tell you. Naturally, I didn't know where the camera was or anything! I was not an actress. I was a schoolgirl. I had never been out of the house without the family. I was around stage actors who knew everything. I had the most wonderful director, George Melford, who used to be the director for Rudolph Valentino. Anyway, they made the English films in the daytime and in the evening, the Spanish group would come in and we would work through the night. Back then, I didn't have a car, so, I had to walk from Universal to Lankershim. From there, I took the streetcar to Hollywood, where I lived with my grandmother in a bungalow

A photo of Lupita signed to her future husband Paul Kohner.
Photo courtesy of Pancho Kohner.

court. When Universal found out, they sent a studio car to come pick me up in the evening and in the morning bring me back home. It was hard, in the daytime. You couldn't sleep with all the daylight, and in those days, people used to hang their carpets outside and bang them, to clean them. God, it was noisy! The studio kind of made me over. The first thing they did was send me to the dentist to check my teeth. The dentist saw I had beautiful teeth. I also started taking English lessons right away. I had to learn a lot, I had to learn to also dance. I took dancing lessons at eight o'clock. I would then take a rest from dancing, and then work. The studio gave me an interpreter, though she was more interested in keeping up her Spanish instead of teaching me English (laughs).

MATT: What did your grandmother think of coming from Mexico to Hollywood?

LUPITA: My grandmother was Irish—Mrs. Sullivan. She came to this country in a covered wagon through El Paso. Her father left her and her sister in a convent in El Paso because his wife had died. They came from Michigan. Later, she married John Douglas Sullivan, and they moved with their family further south. He would go back and forth to El Paso, and on one of those trips, he never came back. My grandmother did not speak Spanish, but she had to do something. She was left with three small children to care for. She worked at night at a hospital, and in the daytime, she used to cook meals for the workers of the railroad. They used to go to Mrs. Sullivan for lunch and her wonderful apple pies. She had to raise a family alone. She never heard from her husband again. He must have gotten killed on the way to El Paso or something. He was never heard from again. Those were some wild days of trouble.

MATT: So, you're a mix? I thought you were a full-blooded Mexican.

LUPITA: My mother's side was *Irish* and my father was *Mexican*. He came from the State of Puebla. His grandparents came from Spain. I am a mixture of Spanish and Irish, and of course, *Mexican*! I'm quite a mixture, which I think is wonderful. I have a very wonderful family.

MATT: I was going to bring up your family later, but since we are on the topic, I want to ask you about them. Your daughter is Academy Award nominee Susan Kohner.

LUPITA: Yes. She learned acting from me. I trained her for *Imitation of Life*; that was one of her first films. I coached her.

MATT: You were clearly a great coach. She was nominated for an Oscar. Not only did Susan go into show business, but so did your grandchildren.

LUPITA: My grandchildren are wonderful. All of them turned out so beautiful.

MATT: Chris Weitz is directing *New Moon*, the second installment in the *Twilight* saga.

LUPITA: That's right. And Paul (Weitz) does the *American Pie* movies.

MATT: You must be very proud.

LUPITA: Oh yes! I have a wonderful family. And Pancho, my son, as you know, became a producer. He did some Charlie Bronson films. The first thing he did was *The Bridge in the Jungle*.

MATT: Did you have any idea your whole family would get involved in show business?

LUPITA: I had no idea. My husband and I took Susan to see her first show. We were sitting in the first row on the isle. The producer of the show started talking to my husband, who by then was an agent. He said he was looking for a new girl to put in his show. Since my husband was a big agent, he said, "Just tell me who and I can get her for you." The producer of the show said you see that girl watching the show, pointing over at Susan. I want a girl like that. My husband, Paul, said, "Oh no you don't, she happens to be my daughter." The next day, the phone rang and they wanted to interview Susan for a role. I said to them, "I'm very sorry, but she is going to school." Susan, who was listening, said, "Mom, mom, please." I told her that her father would kill me. She insisted, "Momma, please!" So, I said okay. I went with her for the interview and she got the role. I used to pick her up at school, bring all her schoolbooks, and in-between shows, she did her homework.

MATT: What does Susan Kohner do these days?

LUPITA: She retired from the business. She does a lot of charity work. She is very, very busy. She reads for the blind. I have never seen anyone as active as she is. I'm very proud of my family. All of them are wonderful.

MATT: Paul Kohner, your husband, was the producer of *The Cat Creeps*. Was it love at first sight?

LUPITA: I was scared to death of him. He was always on set, always looking from behind the camera. I was very scared of him. I didn't speak English well, so, there were a lot of misunderstandings at first. I never dreamt I would end up marrying him.

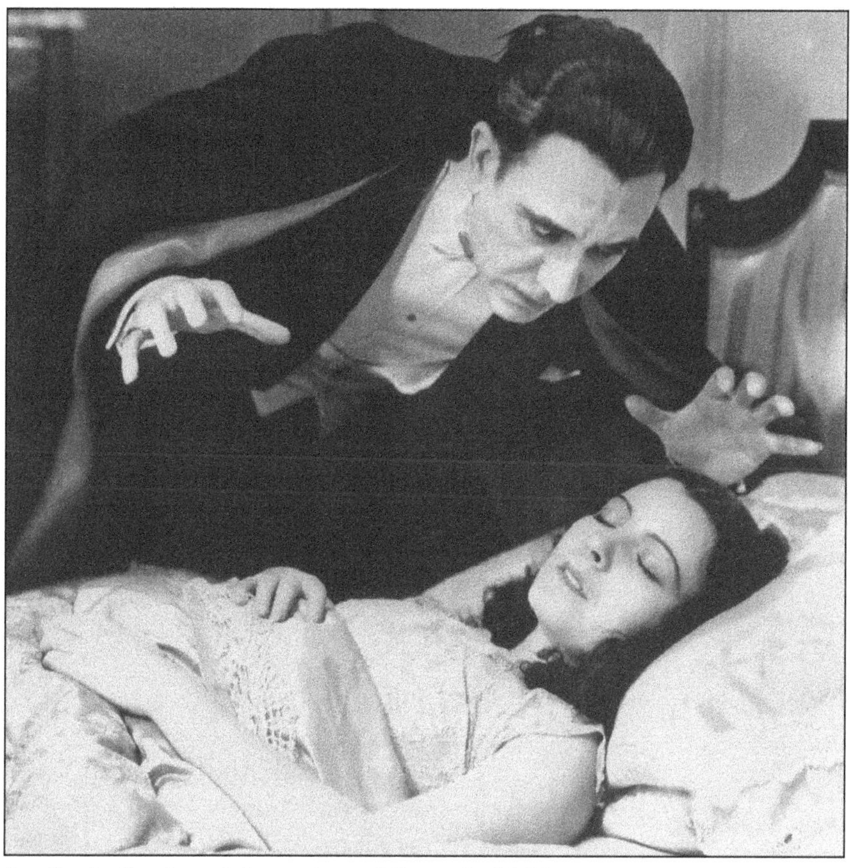

Lupita in the Spanish version of *Dracula* 1931.
Pictured with Carlos Villarias.

Matt: After *The Cat Creeps* came *Dracula*. How did your involvement with Dracula come about?

Lupita: The studio sent me to Mexico with the first film, *The Cat Creeps*, to promote it. It was such a big success that while I was still in Mexico, the studio notified me that I needed to come back immediately and star in a second film, and that film was *Dracula*. While in Mexico, they gave me the title "The Sweetheart of Mexico." I had to appear in every movie theater that was showing the film. I introduced the film to the crowds. I had never done that before.

MATT: Well, you definitely didn't go back to Mexico a failure.

LUPITA: Yes. I was very grateful when people came to see me on my personal appearances. I never prepared a speech. I came out onto the stage and I would talk to the audience. I always thanked the people for being there.

MATT: What was it like when you got back from Mexico promoting *The Cat Creeps*?

LUPITA: Universal could not believe it. I had no contract with them. They sent me on speculation. When I came back from Mexico, they took me to court because, at the time, I was not of age to sign a contract.

MATT: What was it like filming *Dracula*?

LUPITA: I tell you . . . I was scared to death! I still didn't know where the camera was. I knew I was not an actress. The director George Melford, who was the director of *Cat Creeps*, was also directing *Dracula*. He was a very patient and wonderful man. I called him "Uncle George." He took a liking to me. I don't know why I started calling him "Uncle George," but I did. The cast and crew were all wonderful. The head of the electricians was a Mexican man, and his name was Tommy Valdez. Around two o'clock in the morning while shooting, something would drop from the rafters above. It would be a Hershey's bar that Tommy dropped for me. They were wonderful. I was always one hour early. I wanted to be sure and make myself familiar with the set. I would hide in the dark and watch. It was scary sometimes being alone on the set.

MATT: Did you ever run into Bela Lugosi on set?

LUPITA: Oh yes, I met Bela Lugosi many times. He was a very nice man. He was Hungarian. My future husband Paul Kohner, who was a European, was in with all the rest of the show business Europeans. When we started dating, he would invite me to go out for coffee in the afternoon. That's how it was done in those days. You didn't go out for late night dinners. One day Paul asked me if I would like to go with him to the house of Mr. Ernst Lubitsch for afternoon coffee. I went with Paul and that is where I met a lot of the big stars of those days, people like Bela Lugosi, Marlene Dietrich, Greta Garbo, and others. They all spoke German, which I didn't. So, I just sat there quietly listening to them.

MATT: George Melford, who directed the Spanish version of *Dracula*, didn't actually speak a word of Spanish. Was it difficult having a director who didn't speak Spanish?

LUPITA: We had an interpreter and we communicated through him. The script girl also spoke English and Spanish.

MATT: So, you had a couple of people helping with the translation?

LUPITA: Yes.

MATT: Nevertheless, I would still think it created some communication problems.

LUPITA: No, not for me. I was always prepared with my lines. I sat there an hour early and read them. On my first picture, it was different. I did that one, which starred Antonio Moreno, who was a big star of the silent days. When he started doing talkies, he had trouble remembering his lines. He would always blame it on me, saying, "She was this, she was that." Everybody knew it was because he had forgotten Spanish. He had been here in America for a long time doing silent films. His language was no longer right.

MATT: Didn't many members of the cast of *Dracula* come from different Spanish speaking countries?

LUPITA: Yes. We all spoke in a different way, but in real life, that's the way it is. Our grammar and everything is the same. It's just the pronunciation.

MATT: Did you see any differences in the Spanish version from the English version, while you were making the picture?

LUPITA: They had a Moviola on the set. They would watch the English version, and then we had to do exactly what the American actors did. We were not allowed to view the film, only the director and Paul Kohner watched. They would then direct us.

MATT: So, the Spanish cast and crew had a nice head start?

LUPITA: Yes. George Melford and Paul Kohner would change the lighting and everything to making it scarier. They even added more spider webs to enhance its scariness. One day, they showed me the rushes of the day, and I thought the Spanish version was better. In fact, the English version hired Paul Kohner to supervise production on the English version, because our version was so much better. They wanted to know what he did different.

MATT: I agree with you. I think the Spanish version is superior to the American version. I know many cinema buffs agree with that. Isn't it true that the film was lost for a long time?

LUPITA: Yes. They found a copy of the film in Cuba.

MATT: Cuba?

LUPITA: Cuba, of all the places. And then in Washington, they found another. I was happy. The people who had it were so nice. They got in touch with my husband and he was able to get the print.

MATT: When you were filming *Dracula*, did you realize you were making a movie that would have such a cult following after all these years?

LUPITA: No. It was really just a job at the time. As I said, I sent money to my family to keep them alive. I was the oldest of nine children. I put everybody through private school with the money I made.

MATT: You were a good sister.

LUPITA: They were like my children. My youngest sister was seven months old when I left home.

MATT: Are you familiar at all with Carla Laemmle? She is the last cast member from the English version of *Dracula* and is also in this book.

LUPITA: Oh, I met her at the studio. A few years ago, she was brought here to my house, and we did an interview. She is a relative of Carl Laemmle.

MATT: She was his niece.

A still of Lupita in the film _Santa_.

LUPITA: Right. She was in the coach scene in _Dracula_;
            she was one of the girls in the beginning. All the
            relatives of Carl Laemmle were on the payroll at
            Universal. He took care of everybody.

MATT: Another film of yours that I wanted to talk to
            you about was the movie, _Santa_, a truly beautiful
            movie.

LUPITA: _Santa_ was a picture I did in Mexico. It was actually
            the first talkie in Mexico.

MATT: It was a tremendous hit in Mexico, wasn't it?

LUPITA: Oh yeah. They still show it on TV to this day.

MATT: The film was such a hit that the Mexican
          government issued a stamp with your picture on
          it. Isn't that true?

LUPITA: They issued a stamp and also lottery tickets. I
          never thought that would happen. Thank goodness
          it never went to my head. You know, so many
          actresses, once they become famous, they become
          such snobs. I used to walk on the streets and the
          shoe shiners would say, "There goes my sweet-
          heart!" I always turned around and said "Hello."
          I never took myself too serious as a big star. I was
          always grateful for the people who would come
          see me. It's the people that make you a star.

MATT: Do you have a personal favorite film of yours?

LUPITA: I tell you, my favorite is *Santa* because it was the
          first picture I made in Mexico. The story was by
          Federico Gamboa. When I met him, I tell you . . .
          I thought I was going to make a picture about a
          saint, *not a prostitute.*

MATT: The title is misleading. I first thought it was going
          to be a holiday movie.

LUPITA: Have you seen the film?

MATT: Yes.

LUPITA: I played an innocent peasant girl, who becomes the
          most famous prostitute in Mexico. I had no idea.
          When I came home with the book in my hand, my
          father saw it. He said, "That book doesn't come
          into this house."

MATT: What do you make of being a cult figure among
          horror aficionados?

Lupita blowing out the candles at her 99th Birthday.
PHOTO COURTESY OF PANCHO KOHNER.

LUPITA:	I never really thought about it. I still get fan mail from all over the world. A lot from Europe, they show the films on TV there. I still get surprised, usually it gets addressed to my son, and he then brings them to me. They don't realize that I am an old lady almost a hundred years old.
MATT:	Well, Dracula bit your neck. You're going to live forever!
LUPITA:	(Laughs) Yes. You know, they don't make the films like they did those days. The style is different.
MATT:	Do you think the style is worse or better?
LUPITA:	Well, it changed. It changed a lot, let's put it that way.

MATT: Do you watch the films of today?

LUPITA: I go to the Academy all the time. I see the foreign films. I am still very active. I see practically every film that comes out.

MATT: What do you think of them?

LUPITA: Well, it's an entirely different thing. It's not the Hollywood I knew. The style is different. In the old days, it was like a family. Everybody always knew each other. Now you don't. It's too big.

MATT: Why did you retire from moviemaking?

LUPITA: I retired to raise my children. You see, when I was working, I left early in the morning, and came home at night from the studio. By the time I got home, it was time for my children to have a bath, dinner, and bed. I wanted to be close to my family and raise my children. And I tell you . . . I am very happy that I did.

MATT: One of the first things you said in the beginning of the interview was, "I did not want to go back to Mexico a failure." I think it's safe to say that didn't happen. How do you reflect on that?

LUPITA: Now in my old age, I sit back and I say, "My God, did this all happen to me?" To me, it's all like a dream. Today at my age, and with my past, I had a very wonderful life. The producer of *Dracula* and *The Cat Creeps* fell in love with me, and I fell madly in love with him. We were married for so many years. Now, well, I live alone because I choose to be alone. I don't want to move from my house and my garden. I'm still pulling weeds in my garden, which I enjoy. I don't get lonely. I have

Lupita at an event in Los Angeles in 2008.

planted everything outside this house. It was the house that Paul and I built together. When I walk the grounds, I pull the weeds, my mind becomes clear. It's a wonderful feeling nature gives you.

MATT: Gardening sounds like your idea of yoga?

LUPITA: Yes, people say, "Yoga this and yoga that." NO. Gardening is fantastic! You pull weeds, and then you see a new flower grow. It's just wonderful.

MATT: Is there a secret to longevity?

LUPITA: Well, I live a very simple life. I don't go anywhere. I'm in my tennis shoes and my working clothes mostly, and I am in my garden all day long. It keeps my mind clear and happy. My husband and I were very close. When he died, I just retired. I would say it's the gardening that keeps my mind happy. I don't smoke, and I don't drink. Although once in a while, my son comes by and we have a little tequila. Looking back, I had a wonderful life, I have a wonderful family, and more important, I have no regrets. And I just keep on going!

MATT: That's a great note to end this on. Thank you so much, Lupita, for talking to me.

LUPITA: My pleasure, Matthew.

Chapter Three:
JANET ANN GALLOW

As a child actor, Janet Ann Gallow's resume read like a *Who's Who* of a classic era. She is best-remembered to horror fans for her role as Cloestine in *The Ghost of Frankenstein* starring Bela Lugosi and Lon Chaney, Jr.. Miss Gallow was the Little Girl in the Abbott and Costello film, *It Ain't Hay*. Janet also had small roles in *Butch Minds the Baby* starring Broderick Crawford, *Till We Meet Again* starring Ray Milland, *That Night with You* featuring Buster Keaton, and *Canyon Passage* co-starring Dana Andrews, Lloyd Bridges, and Susan Hayward. Quite impressive for only a few years in the business.

Living in Southern California, Janet enjoys her cult status among horror fans. She recently made a cameo appearance in a short film by Wally Wingert titled *Living on a Prayer* co-starring Larry Storch, Stella Stevens, and Chuck McCann. I had the pleasure of interviewing Janet Ann Gallow in Burbank, CA on April 25, 2009.

MATT: You started very young in show business as a child star. Did you want to act?

JANET: My mother was a stage mother. She came to Hollywood with dreams. She decided that she wanted me to be in the pictures. It began with my mother looking for casting agencies. When she got an agent, I started working only, well mostly, at Universal Pictures. I started out in a picture called *Temporary Bride* with just a small, bit part. From there, I was asked to go to some director's office.

At that time, he was looking for a child actress who would not be afraid of Lon Chaney with his Frankenstein monster make up on. So, I went there and was able to get the part. I couldn't read, at the time, because I was only five. My mother and I would go over the script together. Consequently, I began memorizing the part before I would do my scenes. This was all before I worked on the actual set. When I started working on set, Jack Pierce and the other people who made up the monster asked me to come into the dressing room where Lon was being made up. They wanted to see if I would be frightened. I saw him first as a person, and then I saw him as the monster. It didn't bother me. He didn't frighten me at all. In fact, I loved him. He was a great guy.

MATT: What was it like making the movie? Do you have vivid memories of it since you were so young?

JANET: I have great memories! Everybody was very nice to me. I was pretty much the only kid on set. Consequently, they took their time with me. Everyone was kind of playing with me between the different scenes. I had a great time.

MATT: You mentioned Lon Chaney and going to his makeup room. Did you see him get made up?

JANET: I just remember going there and watching people put this greenish looking stuff on his face. Little by little, it would get thicker and thicker, and pretty soon, they put the bolts on the sides of his neck! I just watched and could see how he was transformed at the time.

MATT: Do you remember how long it took to film your scenes?

Janet and Lon Chaney, Jr. in *Ghost of Frankenstein.*

JANET: I was there for about three weeks.

MATT: In a lot of publicity photos for the movie, you're hoisted up on Lon Chaney's shoulder pretty high? Did that intimidate you at all?

JANET: Not a bit. When they did the scene where the ball went up on the roof, they took a doll that was made to look like me up on the roof because they couldn't take me up that high. So, they made this doll. She looked a bit stiff to me, but she was the one up on top of the roof with the ball.

MATT: That was a doll?

JANET: (Laughs with a grin) Yup, that wasn't me. I was probably two feet off the ground. That was about all people saw of me. Then, it cut to the doll.

MATT: Did they take any extra care of you, since you were so young?

JANET: A little. I could only work so many hours on set, and then I would have to be taken off set. There was a certain time limit.

MATT: Did they school you when you were not filming?

JANET: No, I didn't get schooled on the set of *The Ghost of Frankenstein*. Since I was only five years old at the time, I did, however, get schooled on set for other films later on.

MATT: What was it like working with Lon Chaney?

JANET: Oh, he was wonderful. He was terrific and very patient with me. We would go over my lines together. A very nice man. When my mom passed

Janet with Lon Chaney, Jr. and Bela Lugosi in *Ghost of Frankenstein*.

away, I was still very young. Lon Chaney actually offered to adopt me.

MATT: Lon Chaney offered to adopt you? I never knew that.

JANET: Yes, and my brother, who was two at the time.

MATT: How did your mom pass away?

JANET: Pneumonia. She got sick in San Francisco, and she died two weeks later.

MATT: Your mom, you said, was the driving force behind your show business career. With her passing, did that pretty much end your career as a kid actor?

JANET: Yes, pretty much. I did a couple of little things, but my dad couldn't keep up with making a living for the family and taking me out to different studios and such.

MATT: Did you keep in touch with Lon Chaney long after that?

JANET: I did for a little while. I even sent him an invitation to my wedding, but I never got a response. It was quite a few years after I had filmed with him!

MATT: The way you talk about Lon Chaney, it feels as though you looked up to him as a father figure.

JANET: Yes, I did. His wife was very nice to me, a very sweet lady. She always treated me nicely, when I would go to their house.

MATT: Can you tell me more about that?

JANET: When I would go to their house, Patsy had a collection of copper miniatures, and I would always get to play with those. A couple of times, I got lost in their house. It was pretty big.

MATT: The time you spent with Lon Chaney certainly sounds very special to you. Aside from *Ghost of Frankenstein*, you also did *Butch Minds the Baby* with Broderick Crawford. Do you remember that?

JANET: It's very vague for me. My scenes were cut from the movie once we were done filming, anyway.

MATT: You also appeared in a movie with Abbott and Costello called *It Ain't Hay*. What was that experience like?

Janet: Costello was wonderful. Abbot was a bit more stern. I ended up kissing Costello, and also slapping him in the face.

Matt: Really?

Janet: Yeah (laughs).

Matt: Why would you do that?

Janet: Well, because evidently there was a race with a horse. And I gave him a kiss because I wanted him to win the race. Then later, I found out he didn't win, and the horse had died, so I slapped him.

Matt: That is funny. You also did a movie with Buster Keaton.

Janet: What movie?

Matt: *That Night with You.*

Janet: Oh, yes. That was a movie about orphan kids. I was one of the oldest, and I talked more than most of the kids. We were orphans, who came to the house, and I remember being with Susanna Foster. It was a very touching movie about orphan children.

Matt: And another film you did was *Canyon Passage.*

Janet: Yes. I was the older of two other children, and we went on a covered wagon trip, and at some point, Indians were coming at us and they set the wagon on fire!

Matt: Do you wish sometimes that you had continued your career in show business?

Janet at Carla Laemmle's 100th birthday celebration in Hollywood in 2009.
PHOTO BY MATT BECKOFF.

JANET: I don't know, I can't say. I probably would have gone on if my mother had lived. I don't know what life would have held for me at that point. You don't know what's going to happen in life.

MATT: What did you do after acting?

JANET: I went to high school and got married very young. I had a couple of kids, and later divorced (laughs). *[For the record, Janet is currently happily married].* Then started working at Teledyne Technologies in Aerospace for a long time. Then, I went back to school and became a pre-school teacher.

Janet with Carla Laemmle at a 2009 autograph convention.
Photo by Matt Beckoff.

MATT: What do people think of your past life as a child actor in show business when they find out?

JANET: I don't think most of them realize or understand it or are even that interested in it. Only people that have been through that business understand it. Normal people kind of look at you and go, "Whatever."

MATT: Do you remember when the sudden interest in you occurred again?

JANET: Oh yes! It was at a Jack and Jill luncheon at the Sportsman's Lodge in Los Angeles. The person taking care of the sound system at the lodge happened to know of people who were looking for me. So, from there, I started doing autograph shows.

MATT: What do you make of your cult status among horror fans?

JANET: I think it's very fascinating, and fun. I feel very lucky to have been in the movie, *The Ghost of Frankenstein.*

MATT: Is it kind of strange for you going to conventions, signing autographs for fans after being out of show business for that long?

JANET: It is kind of strange. It is. But it's fun. You get to talk to a lot of people who are very much interested in horror films.

MATT: It must be surreal.

JANET: It is!

MATT: You recently did a cameo in a movie by Wally Wingert called *Living on a Prayer.* What was it like being on set after all of those years?

JANET: It was great! It was a lot of fun! Stella Stevens was there. Also Chuck McCann and Larry Storch were part of it! It was a really fun afternoon filming that scene. It felt very easy for me. It didn't seem like work at all. I would love to do more film work.

MATT: I think your fans would love to see you do more work, too. On that note, Janet, I would like to thank you so much for sitting down with me to talk.

JANET: You're welcome. Thank you.

Chapter Four:
ELENA VERDUGO

When I called Elena Verdugo about doing an interview for my book, her first question was, "What's the book about?" I explained to her that it was a book of interviews with actresses who appeared in classic horror movies. Without missing a beat, she said, "I'll never get away from that movie!" She was referring to the Universal horror film, *House of Frankenstein*. Such statements are only a true testament to horror movies and the people who love them. However, Ms. Verdugo does not have to worry. She is also fondly remembered to the public for her role on the television series, *Marcus Welby, M.D.*, a role which garnered her two Emmy nominations. She currently resides in Los Angeles with her husband.

Here is our interview from April 21, 2009.

MATT: I read your family migrated to the Americas back in 1776. Can you tell me briefly about it?

ELENA: Somewhere in that area. My ancestor, Jose Maria Verdugo, was a Sergeant in the Spanish Army. He received a land grant from the King of Spain. They were going to give those who retired here land in California, and Jose came out and looked it over. He liked the Glendale, Burbank area from the Hollywood Bowl to far past Glendale. It was 36,000 acres of land. He brought brothers, sisters, and had a lot of sons. They were just happy farmers, rancheros, and they didn't like it at all when the

Americans started coming in. I had that initial grant he had. I recently donated it to the Glendale library. They have a Verdugo section. I had some other papers that showed the land. There's a bit of history there. I always joke, "We had all this land. Where is it now?" It's become the city of Glendale. They still have the first Verdugo house up in Glendale. They also have Verdugo day.

MATT: Fascinating. I know there is a lot of history there, but I would like to focus mainly on your career. How did you get your start dancing in films?

ELENA: Well, if you can call it a start. I was very young, about five or six. They needed a little Spanish dancer for the film, *Cavalier of the West*. I don't even remember auditioning or anything. I just showed up on set. The film starred Harry Carey. The cast was all real sweet to me. I have since learned that *Cavalier of the West* was one of the first talkies. Then, I did a couple of little things here and there. The big start was at about fifteen years of age, and they needed a Spanish dancer for *Down Argentine Way* with Betty Grable. I had to audition for this one. I went to 20th Century Fox, to their big rehearsal hall, where they had their own pianist. So, I danced for Nick Castle, who was one of the biggest choreographers in the business. He was so excited about my work that he started calling other producers in to see my dancing. After that, I got the part. I guess I looked pretty good. I mean, who doesn't look good at fifteen? Next thing I knew, Betty Grable, who was a sweetheart to me, called up this big agent and told them all about me. She wanted to give me a helping hand, the dear lady. Next thing I knew, I was under contract and going to school at 20th Century Fox. My classmates were Anne Baxter, June Haver, Roddy

A glamorous Elena.

McDowall, Stanley Clements, my girlfriend Joan Leslie, and Harold Nicholas of The Nicholas Brothers. He and I would dance at recess. Everyone else killed time. He and I would turn on the radio and dance away.

MATT: What a sight that must have been! What were some other early roles?

ELENA: Probably my best and nicest credit was at sixteen in *The Moon and Sixpence*. It was about Paul Gauguin, a famous painter. George Sanders played the man, and I played the native girl that he takes as his little wife. It was a wonderful part and a great experience. I'm not sure that I didn't have my sixteenth birthday during filming on set. After that, I went to work for Paramount studios. Cecil DeMille wanted me for a film he was doing. Two weeks before production, he changed his mind and thought this other young lady was better for the part. I must have still been a minor though, because I was still going to school on the set.

MATT: Were the schools any good?

ELENA: No. They were terrible. The schools were awful. They were nice people and all. The teacher at Paramount never showed up. She was quite a character. There was a younger lady, too. She had been Shirley Temple's private tutor. They would assign us all teachers when we were on the set. When you're on the set, you still have to have three hours schooling. When I was doing *The Moon and Sixpence*, I had a very dramatic scene. The teacher, a male teacher, didn't like giving his students too much work when they had to film dramatic scenes. I got off a little easy there.

MATT: Soon after that, you appeared in *House of Frankenstein.*

ELENA: Well, when I left Paramount. Actually they dropped me. Then *House of Frankenstein* came along. I don't remember auditioning. I don't remember meeting anyone. I just know the next thing I knew, I was in it. In the wardrobe department, they were hooking me up to this girdle thing. In *The Moon and Sixpence*, I wore a beautiful long wig that had been Loretta Young's. In real life, I had light brown hair. In this Universal film, I wore a black wig done by Max Factor. I can't tell you how many black wigs I wore in countless pictures. Once you get typed that's it. It was fun though.

MATT: Did you find you were getting typecast early on?

ELENA: I was a song and dance girl at heart. I love all the musicals. However, I didn't get to perform in many. But in a lot of those pictures, I did have a dance scene. I can't tell you how many times I did that same dance. They would always introduce me right in the middle of the dance, never the whole thing. I thought, *Gosh, how come I didn't change the steps?* And I realized, I never thought anyone was looking at them!

MATT: That's how you are introduced in *House of Frankenstein*, dancing.

ELENA: Yes. That's what I had done in *Down Argentine Way*, and in a Gene Autry picture called *Big Sombrero*, where I played a fiery Mexican.

MATT: Do you remember the filming of the movie *House of Frankenstein?*

Elena with Lon Chaney, Jr. in *House of Frankenstein*.

ELENA: We shot at Universal. Then, we shot the wagon
scene on location at night. That was great fun.
It's the first time I ever acted in a movie. All of a
sudden, they just let me go. I thought to myself,
Don't they want to direct me? I thought, *You're
supposed to have a lot of direction. What's going on?*
But they just put the camera on me, put the lights
on me, and we went. That was in the back of the
caravan. I worked that scene with J. Carroll Naish,
who, interestingly enough, was in the same scene I
did in *Down Argentine Way*. Here we were several
years later in *House of Frankenstein*.

MATT: Interesting. You said it was fun doing the carriage
scene. Could you elaborate?

ELENA: It was a real carriage. It had a feeling of great authenticity. A lot of the movie felt that way. I never felt embarrassed by anything. However, a little bit towards the end, that crawling scene was a little hammy. By and large, I felt the presence of some very superior actors on the set.

MATT: Lon Chaney Jr. being one of them. What was it like working with him?

ELENA: He was a doll. He was aware that I was a younger girl. He would always ask if I wanted something to drink. He was just charming. We would go out to his wagon, off the set, and I would pop myself up on it. He would have a beer and I would have a Coke. There he was in his makeup and I was in my outfit. He told me about where he lived in the Valley. He was also curious about the Verdugos. Lon Chaney broke the ice. Not so much with the others. They were not interested in talking to an eighteen-year-old girl. Lon was just darling. One time, a cameraman came up to where we were and he wanted to see us together. I lifted up one of Lon's wolf claws and pretended I was filing it. We had some real fun together.

MATT: Do you remember seeing Lon Chaney transform from himself into the Wolf Man?

ELENA: I know it took a lot of time, several hours. It was done in stages. His hands were always in gloves and the feet were covered wearing boots, all of which had fur. I will tell you one thing: I did not see him completely in his Wolf Man outfit until we had to do a scene together. He was off getting made up by himself. They weren't even going to have us do a rehearsal of it. It was a simple shot. He had to burst through the door, and I scream.

Elena with Lon Chaney, Jr. as The Wolf Man in *House of Frankenstein*.

Then he goes out, and I shoot him, then I crawl to him. The studio hired a professional screamer to let out a big scream for the shot. Well, when he burst into the room and I turned around and saw him in that outfit, I let out the loudest scream—so loud they used it in the film! They didn't use the professional they had hired. When they told me about the professional screamer I laughed. I thought that was kind of cute.

MATT: What was it like working with Boris Karloff?

ELENA: I tell you, I felt in the company of Mr. Boris
          Karloff. I was young at the time, so he didn't have
          much to say to me. He wasn't rude, but he was
          aloof. There was something about him. He had this
          magnetism. Even though I was a teenager, I knew
          he was a very special person. He wasn't a fellow
          actor. He was Mr. Karloff.

MATT: Sounds like he had a strong presence?

ELENA: Yes indeed. But there was something so quiet about
          him. He just sat there with his tea.

MATT: We all know Bela Lugosi as the original Dracula.
          Do you know why Bela Lugosi didn't reprise his
          role as Dracula in *House of Frankenstein*?

ELENA: No. Isn't that a shame? That would have been
          wonderful. I think he was sick sometimes. He had
          his demons. I've heard more about him in later
          years. My husband is a psychiatrist and he was
          connected to the mental hospital in Norwalk. I
          think there was a time when Mr. Lugosi was receiving
          treatments there. Isn't that too bad? Either he was
          born with it, or the movies drove him crazy.
          During my era, everyone was in analysis trying to
          find out more about themselves. And before that, I
          guess, nobody knew anything. I only stayed with
          people who were fun. I never had a desire to be
          with people who were deeply involved.

MATT: Does it surprise you after all these years that people
          still remember you for *House of Frankenstein*?

ELENA: I had no idea. I had no idea while we were doing
          it. I wasn't particularly a fan of that type of work. I

was young and somewhat embarrassed. I wanted to do movie musicals. I wouldn't tell anyone about *House of Frankenstein*. And yet, it has survived my career. It will be shown long after I'm gone. There are certain things that turn out to be somewhat of a classic. It's not a great film, but it was put together rather well.

MATT: Universal did a good job producing those horror movies.

ELENA: They did. Didn't they?

MATT: Were you a fan of the Universal horror movies?

ELENA: No. But I'm enjoying it now. I can see the humor to it. I couldn't when I was young. I just thought, *Oh it's a way to make money and there's an audience for it.* But I was very narrow-minded. I just liked pretty things and pretty costumes. I really wanted to do more movie musicals.

MATT: You also appeared in *The Frozen Ghost* with Lon Chaney?

ELENA: I keep calling it "*The Tummy Ghost.*" It's *The Frozen Ghost.* It's sometimes hard to remember. I wasn't very good. I'm not too proud of myself for not taking things more seriously. I didn't know who this character was in the film. I didn't know what to do with her. And here I am with a name as an actress. I didn't really know anything about acting. I hadn't studied acting. I studied dancing. Instinct got me through, and little by little, you teach yourself and you watch other performers, especially those that you admire.

MATT: Whom do you admire?

ELENA: Most of them are men. I loved the good ones.

MATT: Is it true Universal Studios didn't treat you well?

ELENA: Oh, that's sort of a publicity thing. Right after the horror pictures, I did an Abbott and Costello film. It was cute and I had fun doing it. Back then, I was, shall we say, pleasantly plump. I don't know why being thin didn't seem important to me. As I said, I was self-centered and young. I didn't know how to diet and I didn't want to. My husband, at the time, was a writer. He had close ties with the studio. He said to me once, "You know they would make a star of you, if you would just lose some weight." I thought to myself, 'Oh, really?' That went in one ear and out the other. Thank God, television came along and I jumped in. I auditioned and got this part on *Meet Millie*. I think of myself as a performer and not an actress. I can perform and make things happen. I was able to use those skills because it was live television then. As we'd perform it in Los Angeles, they'd see it in New York. I just heard from Marvin Kaplan, actually. He and I are the only survivors from the cast. Had it not been for *Meet Millie*, I would have gone on playing gypsy girls until I started playing gypsy moms!

MATT: Most people recognize you best from your role as Consuelo Lopez on the television series *Marcus Welby, M.D.* Did you enjoy doing the series?

ELENA: Well, that's what they say! That feels like yesterday, but it was over thirty years ago. It was a wonderful experience. I was a little teed off because here I was back to playing an ethnic part. She was a Mexican-American. But I had fun with that because I had grown up! When I was a young blonde and swinging,

A photo of Elena and author Matt Beckoff taken after the interview for this book.

it was foreign to me playing ethnic parts. *Foreign*. But when I got *Marcus Welby M.D.*, I was more knowledgeable. I even added more to the character as far as Latin characteristics, more than they had asked me to do.

MATT: Your character was a breakthrough for Latino women. There were not many role models for Latino women back then on TV, right?

ELENA: No. There was not. That's why it did a lot of good. There was a big Hispanic movement at the time. I am honored to have been there. In fact, I have a friend who once said, "Elena, I didn't know what to do with my life. I have children. My marriage has broken up. What am I going to do? And I watched you on *Marcus Welby, M.D.* It inspired me to become a nurse." She identified with my character being Latin. Many people have told me that I inspired them to become nurses. It's wonderful.

MATT: You also have a star on the Hollywood Walk of Fame. That must be a thrill?

ELENA: It's been there a long time. I just love it! I have more fun with that than anything. When I tell people that I have a star on Hollywood and Vine, they light up. When I got my star, I was told through a letter in the mail. It was in the early years of the Hollywood Walk. I didn't get a big hoop-de-do ceremony like they do today.

MATT: What is life like today for you?

ELENA: It's very serene. I work hard at that.

MATT: Wonderful. Thank you for your time, Elena. It's been a pleasure.

Chapter Five:
COLEEN GRAY

Coleen Gray, in my opinion, is one of the most underappreciated stars of Hollywood's Golden Era. Having started out early in her career working with some of the biggest names in Hollywood, such as John Wayne and Frank Capra, Coleen was soon released from her Fox studio contract. Being dropped from a major studio is usually the end to an actor's career, but not for Coleen. Her talent and her beauty, a beauty that might have actually *kept* her from landing more meaty roles, nevertheless kept Coleen busy in films and television for decades. She is best known for her work in the *film noir* classics *Kansas City Confidential, Kiss of Death, Nightmare Alley*, and Stanley Kubrick's *The Killing*. Horror fans also know her for her work in the movie *The Vampire* with John Beal and her starring role in *The Leech Woman*. Here is our interview done shortly after New Year's 2010.

MATT: Can you tell me about where you are from, Coleen?

COLEEN: I was born in Nebraska, that's in the United States, on a farm in Staplehurst, Nebraska. Population was about ninety. I lived there till I was about six, when we moved to Minnesota, another cold place. I don't like the cold and I don't like snow. That white stuff, I grew up in it. I don't want to be around it anymore. It's very pretty on mountains. It's nice taking pictures of a snowcapped mountain, but I don't want to ski on it. No way José.

MATT: When did you know you wanted to be an actress?

COLEEN: That was in junior high school in Hutchinson, Minnesota. My older brother was no company, so I read a lot of books. The neighbors had movie magazines and they would loan them to me. I would read them all. I became enamored by the lifestyle and the beauty of the actors and actresses I saw pictured. I thought, *I want to look like them. I want to be a movie star.* It wasn't so much the acting; it was probably an escape from the farm and the solitude. My English teacher, Miss Bisel, went around the class one day and said, "What are your ambitions? What do you want to do when you grow up?" Most girls wanted to be a secretary, a teacher, a nurse, or a housewife. I said, "I want to be a movie star." Well, the whole class erupted in laughter, and I never said that again. I was sensitive. I did nothing to further that goal. I just pushed it down.

MATT: Did you do the school plays?

COLEEN: Yes. Whenever there was a play, I was in it. I remember in that same period we did *The Tempest* and I had the part of Sycorax the witch. That was one of my first memories of the plays I was in.

MATT: When did you decide to leave for Los Angeles?

COLEEN: I went to college on a scholarship, and during college, we went into World War II. I worked my way through college as a waitress, in addition to the scholarship, but I had no training for anything. I planned on being a public school music teacher. I took some classes in education and they bored the heck out of me. I couldn't bear it. They can really kill your ambition with those boring classes. Anyway, my fiancé was in the Army stationed at Camp Callan in Southern California near La Jolla. I had just graduated Summa Cum Laude from Hamline University, class of 1943. I had no career in mind whatsoever. I was qualified to do nothing but wait tables. So, I took a Greyhound bus to visit him. That's how I got to California, La Jolla specifically.

MATT: What happened once you got to La Jolla?

COLEEN: I got a place to live in a dormitory for wives and sweethearts of servicemen. I got a job as a waitress in a very fine hotel restaurant. There I was again, as a waitress, but I earned my keep. After about six weeks of that, I realized I had to do something. I came to Los Angeles and stayed with my mother's best friend, Hannah Jensen. I had developed a social conscience at Hamline and wanted to save the world. Soon, we set about finding something for me to do. She knew Grace Steinbeck, a cousin of author John Steinbeck. She was the General Secretary of the YWCA. We thought that the YWCA, which was a social service organization, might have some place for this young idealist. They gave me a job at $60 a month as a typist. I am not a typist, I am not a secretary. I did not know shorthand, but it was a job. I will never forget the aches in my shoulder from being hunched up to my ears with tension, as I made mistake after mistake in those letters. It was a long, dreadful occupation. I went to night school to learn short hand so that I could improve my station in life at the YWCA. Typing letters did not seem to me to be really saving the world. I was rather discouraged, so I looked in the want ads of the Los Angeles Times. I saw a little ad that read "Casting *Letters to Lucerne*." I called and got the address. I knocked on the door. The door opened and there was Carl

Heins Roth. He had bulbous eyes, a wild head of black curly hair, and a pale face. He had been an assistant to Max Reinhardt in Vienna. He had a little theater group in Los Angeles. I auditioned for him and he gave me the lead in the play, *Letters to Lucerne*. I had appeared in that play during college. In college, I had the second lead. Now I had the first lead! I was thrilled beyond belief, only to be brought down to earth by the daunting information that little theaters charge tuition, and this little theater cost $20 a month, and I was only making $60 a month. Nevertheless, I signed on. I lived penuriously, which was not a new experience since I grew up during the Depression. I was a penny pincher, even though we didn't have many pennies to pinch. I had what I now consider a marvelous education in learning to save money and learning how to get by. The experience of being in the little theater was just magnificent. These little theaters were showcases for the Hollywood talent scouts, who would be looking for new faces to bring to the attention of the studios.

MATT: Is that how you were discovered?

COLEEN: So to speak. That talent scout from Fox did not find me there, but that's the way my agent found me. An agent named Jack Pomeroy discovered me. I was signed to a contract that said he would represent me. So, now we come to the time the agent takes me out to Twentieth Century Fox. We went to the casting department and I sat on a bench. Jack said, "Wait here for me," and he disappeared. I'm sitting there waiting, and a man comes along and is about to go into his office. He turned around and said, "Are you waiting to see me?" I said, "I don't know?" (laughs). He asked me what I was doing there, so I told him. He then

Coleen and Tyrone Power in *Nightmare Alley*.

asked me to come into his office. It turns out he was the assistant to the head of the casting department. He asked me a lot of questions, and I'm thinking, *What's going on? Where's my agent?* Finally, this man says, "Follow me." So, I followed him to the head of the casting department. We went into this office, a very big office, and there were several people lined up, about five or six gentlemen. My agent was among them, sweating. At the end of the room, there was a huge desk behind which sat a man who looked like a bulldog. His name was Rufus Le Maire, head of casting. He was ugly. As a matter of fact, I digress for a minute to tell you this little story. In those days, the casting people would go to Pasadena and catch the train to go to New York City to look for new faces on Broadway. One evening, somebody saw Rufus on the platform waiting for the train and said "Hey Rufus, where you going?" Rufus said, "I'm going to New York to look for new faces." The gentleman says, "While you're there, get one for yourself." (Laughs). Anyway, this man pounded on the desk and he says, "You're an actress huh? You act? Let's see you act?" My agent's eyes were popping out of his head. We were not ready for this. I did a quick think and thought about *Brief Music*, this play I had just done. In it I had a page monologue, a happy jubilant sort of speech, which I did. Then I went into another page of Act 3, a monologue in which I was crying and depressed. I cried real tears. Rufus then pounded at the desk and said "Ivan! Why haven't you brought this girl in?" That was Ivan Kahn who was the head talent scout at Fox Studios. So, that's how I got discovered. That was July 14th of 1944, Bastille Day.

MATT: That is a great story.

COLEEN: They made a contract between Fox and me. That contract basically said Fox had first dibs on me and that they would test me, and that no other studio had any permission. It didn't say when they would test me and there was no money involved. They just had "dibs." So, I quit my job at the Y and sat at the phone waiting to be tested. Good luck! (Laughing).

MATT: When did they finally screen test you?

COLEEN: The test actually occurred on October 16th 1949. In the meantime, I got a job at Thrifty drug store as an evening clerk. I made 25¢ an hour. However, I am not mathematically inclined. I am a right brain, not a left. Many nights when I would check out, I was several dollars ahead and the owners pocketed that money. The poor customers got cheated. If I were under, they took it from my salary. I would sometimes end up working for nothing. Too bad, baby! That was not very profitable. Then, I worked at the Farmers Market with the condition that when the screen tests for Fox came along, I could take off. Eventually, they got around to testing me, and the test scene was an adaptation of a scene from *Green Grow the Lilacs*, which was made into a musical called *Oklahoma*. The young man at Fox who wrote the screen test was Rod Amateau. The day we did the test, I could do no wrong. I felt like I had swallowed an electric light bulb. When Darryl F. Zanuck saw the test, they signed me. I was accepted. I became a contract player. My starting salary was $125 a week. Whoopee!

MATT: Was *Kiss of Death* your first film?

COLEEN: No. Before that, I did *Red River* with John Wayne. *Red River* didn't come out till 1948, but it was filmed years before.

MATT: How was it working with John Wayne?

COLEEN: Well you're getting the cart before the horse. You're missing out on a delicious story. How did you get that part?

MATT: Right. How did you get the part in the movie?

COLEEN: Okay. Well, my agent Jack Pomeroy took me to see a man named Howard Hawks. By now, I had married Rod Amateau, who wrote the screen test at Fox, and we had a child. I was married in August 1945; my daughter was born June 1946. This was roughly August or September of 1946. So, they put me on layoff and gave the part to somebody else. Anyway, so here we are in fall of 1946. My agent takes me to see Howard Hawks. Now, I don't know Howard Hawks. The name means nothing to me. I was not up on all that movie stuff. I was still the farm girl from Minnesota. They had been looking for a girl to play the part of Fen in the beginning of *Red River.* They had interviewed either 300 or 3,000 applicants. I love thinking it was 3,000, but it was probably 300. I talked to Mr. Hawks in great length. He was an interesting man. One could really talk to him. He said, "Okay, you have to lower your voice a couple of octaves. If you could lower your voice a couple of octaves we will test you next week." He loved Lauren Bacall, and all the husky-voiced *femme fateles*. He told me to spend the weekend going out in the hills someplace screaming till my voice broke. And I said, "Yes sir." *Over my dead body*, I thought to myself, and I didn't. However, I did test and I spoke as low as I possibly could. To make a long story short, he chose me. It was good news—with one exception. My agent did not get permission to take me to see Howard Hawks. He had not asked Ben Lyon, successor to Rufus Le Maire, or any of the people in the chain of command at Fox to take me, this girl, this nonentity they were doing nothing with. To punish Mr. Pomeroy, he was barred from the lot, and I was refused permission to do the film. I was in deep disgrace. My husband, Rod, said, "In this kind of situation, you go to the top." The top was Darryl Zanuck. I made an appointment with Darryl Zanuck to explain the situation and ask his permission. I got an appointment to see him. I was a little scared. I had heard he was a womanizer. I wouldn't know what to do if he made a pass. It scared the heck out of me. This is a true story. Judy

Holliday went to see him once, and he made a pass at her, and she pulled out a falsie and said, "Here, pet this." (Laughs). A falsie was a fake breast. Anyway, at the beginning of our meeting I said, "Glad to meet you, Mr. Zanuck. You're from Wahoo, Nebraska. I'm from Staplehurst, Nebraska." That put us on a friendly footing. I told him the whole story. He was very attentive and very pleasant. He said, "Well, if Howard will call me and ask me for you, we'll see what happens." Howard Hawks and Darryl Zanuck played croquet and polo together; that's what those boys did. I got home, and I got on the phone to Mr. Hawks's office and talked to his secretary, Helen. I told Helen, "Darryl said if Howard will call me . . . ." Howard called Darryl, and Darryl said yes. That's how I got the part in *Red River*.

MATT:

What was it like working on a film with John Wayne?

COLEEN:

It was wonderful. We were on location in Elgin, Arizona. It was raining badly, so we all sat in our tents for a while. I wrote out about five pages of what I thought the character Fen's life had been like up until the point she asks John Wayne to "Take me with you." I went through the rain to Mr. Hawks's tent and knocked on the door. I gave him the papers and said, "Would you please read this? This is what I think Fen was like." He took them and thanked me. I'm sure he got a kick out of that.

MATT:

In 2008, the American Film Institute named *Red River* the fifth greatest Western picture ever made. Did you know that?

COLEEN:

No I did not. But it was a darned good movie. Borden Chase wrote a good screenplay. Let's face it.

They had a good screenplay, a great director, and good actors. I call that the Holy Trinity. You have to have those three ingredients.

MATT: Did Fox welcome you back with open arms?

COLEEN: No, they didn't. I was *persona non grata* in the casting department because I went over their heads right up to Darryl Zanuck. When you do that, you draw enmity from the underlings. Nothing happened because *Red River* took forever to get out. Nobody saw it or knew anything about it. Meanwhile, nothing was happening with me. A few months later, Rod Amateau brought home a book from Twentieth Century Fox called *Nightmare Alley* by William Lindsay Gresham. He said, "Read this." I did. I knew I was born to play Molly. I knocked on Darryl Zanuck's door; it was interview number two with Mr. Zanuck. I told him that I was born to play Molly. He was nice about that, and said, "If we get a big name for Stan Carlisle, we can float an unknown for Molly. If we get a middle-class name, then we have to have three big names for the women. Do you understand that?" I said, "Yes, I do." Mr. Zanuck didn't initially want Tyrone Power in the role since he was a pretty boy. It was a messy role, but Tyrone wanted to prove himself as an actor.

MATT: Before *Nightmare Alley* came out, you did *Kiss of Death*. How and when did *Kiss of Death* come about?

COLEEN: In early 1947, Henry Hathaway was casting *Kiss of Death*. One Friday afternoon, Rod and I went for a weekend to the desert, and his parents took care of our daughter, Susie. About an hour after we left, the phone started ringing. Hathaway wanted to see me. Nobody knew where I was. Hathaway had to go back to New York on Saturday. When I got home Sunday afternoon, everybody said, "You are in trouble. All hell has broken loose." I was again in deep, deep trouble in the casting department. I had not asked permission to leave town. I remember the head of casting, Ben Lyon, saying to me "Hey! Betty Grable doesn't even go to the bathroom without asking permission!" Anyway, they said I lost the chance of a lifetime. Henry has gone back to New York. Eventually, Henry did come back and still wanted to see me. I dressed for the part, met him, and I got the part.

MATT: That was filmed in New York City, right?

COLEEN: Yes. It was on location in New York. It was one of those black and white semi-documentaries. The term *Film Noir* had not been invented at the time. The term was semi-documentary. That was my first trip to the Big Apple.

MATT: What was that like for a country girl?

COLEEN: I walked everywhere. I looked up at all the buildings. I did everything any tourist would do. I was so thrilled. It was such a privilege.

MATT: *Kiss of Death* was Richard Widmark's first movie. What was he like?

COLEEN: I never got to work with him.

MATT: I know you shared no scenes in the movie, but what was he like on set?

COLEEN: I did meet him on set. I heard that laugh. It was naturally the way he laughed. He was a good

Norwegian. He was absolutely sensational in that movie. During that movie, Fox told me that Tyrone Power was doing *Nightmare Alley* and that I could be Molly if I renewed my contract for the same amount of money. When option time comes, your money is supposed to hike up. It was our agreement. They chose to abrogate it by saying, "You can't have this part unless you stay at the same money." I was very upset about that. It was not honorable. It wasn't so much the money as it was the honor and Fox's honor was going down the tube. I said, "No. I will honor the contract as written." Fox actually sent somebody to New York to threaten me. I cried a lot. It was while I was filming *Kiss of Death* and it upset my equilibrium. However, I stuck to my guns. I was very, very mournful. It meant giving up the part I was born to play. I stuck to it and they caved. They let me be Molly and honored the contract.

MATT: Did you enjoy doing *Nightmare Alley* with Fox?

COLEEN: I loved every minute of it. I was so honored. Back in the high school days when I read those movie magazines, I fell in love with Loretta Young and Tyrone Power, the two most beautiful people in Hollywood. I thought Loretta Young was so graceful. I loved that long neck, and her graceful mannerisms. And of course, "Ty." He was the most handsome person that has ever come out of Hollywood. He had a marvelous personality and was very kind. I was awestruck working with him, and here I am married, I have a child, and I'm working with my crush, my big crush! It was wonderful.

MATT: You said that you were born to play Molly in *Nightmare Alley*. Can you tell me why?

COLEEN: We both had naiveté. She had street smarts, but she was basically a pure soul.

MATT: Did you learn how to do any vaudeville acts while preparing?

COLEEN: No. I didn't have to. I wore the costume, stood up in front of a crowd, but it was all special effects. I never did any of it.

MATT: Despite these great films, you soon left Fox studios. Correct?

COLEEN: Fox left me. They decided not to exercise the option and they let me go. I think that was in 1950. I thought that was the end of the world and that I was a total failure. I was a mass of insecurity and depended on agents. I didn't go out and try to find parts on my own. I didn't have that much moxie. Whether it was an "A" picture or a "B" picture didn't bother me. It could be a Western movie, a Sci-Fi film. A job was a job. You did the best with the script that you had. It doesn't matter what category you're in. You do your best.

MATT: You appeared in another classic *film noir* film, *The Killing*, directed by Stanley Kubrick. What was he like as a director? I have heard he can be hard on his actresses.

COLEEN: I was looking forward to that. I went to see *Killer's Kiss*, which he directed. I was impressed with that film. He had a reputation as being a great director. We did our scenes, and he didn't make any suggestions to me. I thought, *What's wrong here? Direct me, Mr. Kubrick. Tell me something. I want to be my best. What have you got to tell me?* He said nothing. I was so depressed. He worked with Marie Windsor.

Coleen and John Beal in *The Vampire*.

Marie should have gotten an Academy Award. I think that is one of the great injustices in Hollywood. She should have gotten more recognition for her work in *The Killing*.

MATT: Maybe you were so good you didn't need direction?

COLEEN: Oh sure. (Laughs).

MATT: You appeared in the horror movie, *The Vampire* (1960). How did that come about?

COLEEN: My agent called. I said, "Fine." I was happy about it. I didn't try out for it or anything. They just picked me.

MATT: Did you enjoy doing a horror picture?

COLEEN: Yes, and I liked working with John Beal. We had a little song we sang. (Coleen sings). "D'ye ken John Beal at the break o' day? D'ye ken John Beal with his coat so gay? D'ye ken John Beal when he's far, far away? With his hounds and his horn in the morning?" John Peel is the real name in the song. It's an English hunting song.

MATT: What was John Beal like?

COLEEN: John was a highly intelligent person. We had good conversations. I hadn't seen that movie for a long time. I saw it a couple of years ago, and I was impressed. I felt so bad for John's character. He didn't mean to be a monster. It was tragic.

MATT: Another horror movie fans remember you for was *The Leech Woman.*

COLEEN: Yes. That was a fun time. I think we shot that thing in five days. It was such a hokey script. The pineal gland is in the middle of your head some place, and to think this dumb ring plunging into the back of somebody's neck is going to penetrate the pineal and then mix that glandular fluid with the sacred Nipe formula, and you ingest it to become young (laughs)! It was so corny, but we all had such fun with it. When it came time to shoot the scenes, we had to sober up. One of the funniest times is when John Van Dreelan, who helped me escape from the jungle, got his in the quicksand. The fake quicksand was water with chopped cork on the top of it. And I had to push his head under it. Quicksand doesn't work that way. The stupidity of it all would be so overwhelming that it was really tough to get serious.

Coleen as the Leech Woman.

That was a challenge for me, trying to be serious pushing his head underwater.

MATT: As an actress did you relate to June's character wanting to stay young?

COLEEN: Oh sure. All women want to stay young. Besides which, you always think wrinkles are coming. I now look like a Leech Woman. I am eighty-seven. You have to expect that sort of thing. One of the biggest compliments that I ever got was from a famous critic named Pauline Kael. She reviewed *The Leech Woman*, saying it was "a ridiculous movie," but she said that "Coleen Gray acts with utter sincerity." From her, it was a tremendous compliment.

MATT: What were the prosthetics on your face?

COLEEN: Oh, that's terrible! They put lens paper on me. Lens paper is this thin paper they put on my face with liquid adhesive. It made for great wrinkles. Around the mouth, you couldn't smile, otherwise it would crack. I remember having to go to lunch and not being able to eat. I think I had a malt beverage that I drank through a straw. I just couldn't eat. It took an hour and a half to put the makeup on and an hour and a half to get it off. My favorite scene in the movie was where I am in my pearls and diamonds and I go up Mulholland Drive with this gentleman. He attempts to strangle me for the pearls, and I get him in the back of the neck with that dumb ring (laughs).

MATT: Do you have a favorite film of yours?

COLEEN: *Red River, Kiss of Death, Nightmare Alley*, and that precious picture, *Riding High* with Bing Crosby that dear Frank Capra directed. I bet you have never seen that.

MATT: No. I honestly haven't.

COLEEN: Too bad, baby! Working with Frank Capra was such a privilege. After we wrapped, I went into mourning. I cried for a week. That picture was the happiest period for me. Frank Capra was such an incredible human being.

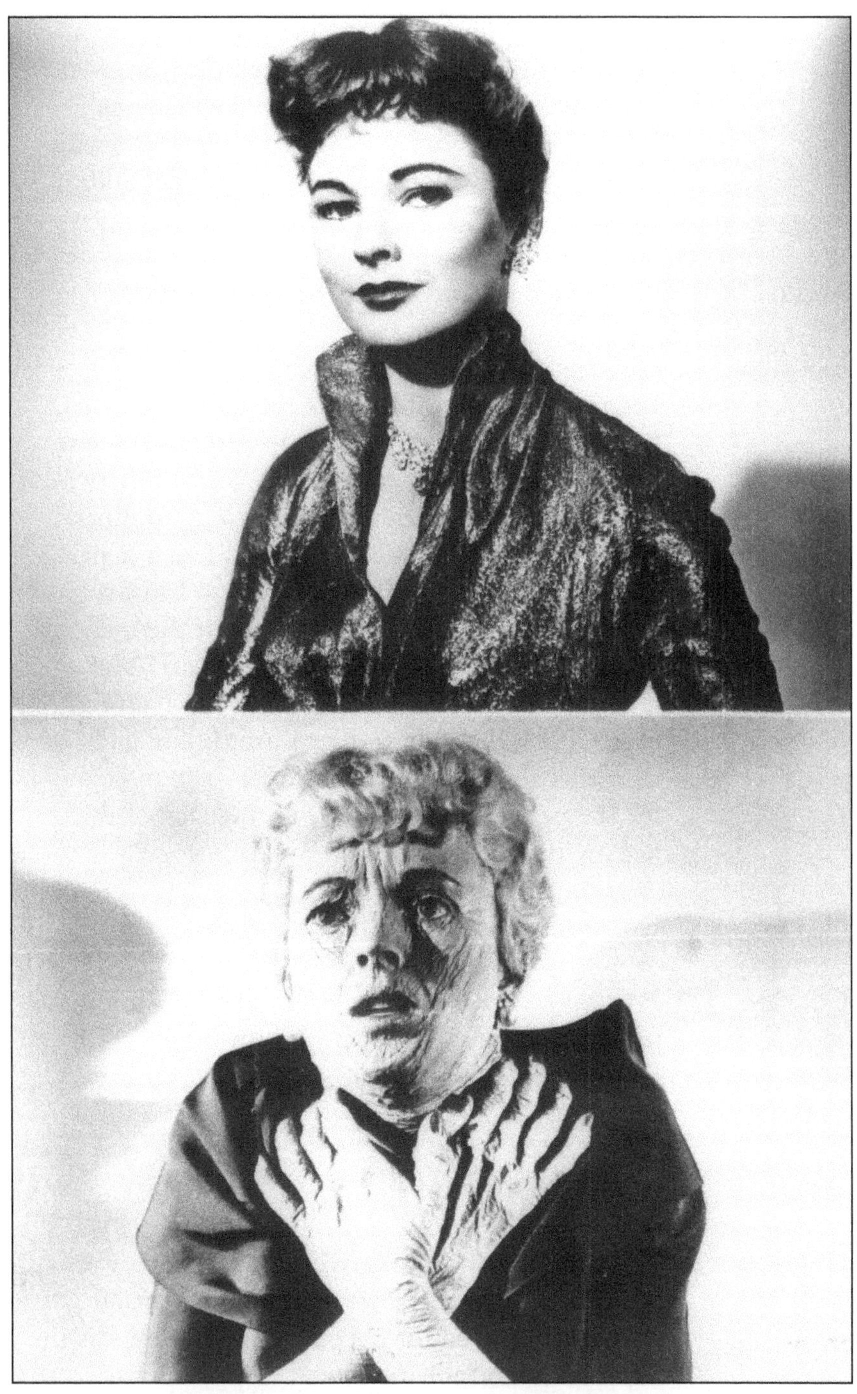

A before and after photo of Coleen getting made up as the Leech Woman.

MATT: Have you ever felt under-appreciated in the business? For one thing, you deserve a Lifetime Achievement Oscar.

COLEEN: Bless your heart. I would settle for a star on the boulevard, but it's a commercial thing nowadays. One year, there was a campaign for me, and they gave it to Zippo, the lighter, instead—a cigarette lighter. I was once referred to as "the stripped gear of the star system."

MATT: When and why did you retire?

COLEEN: They were no longer asking for me. Recently, I have been asked for. It's nice, but I have a problem with my eyes. I can't stand too much light. I would love to see the statistics on the number of women who worked on location with reflectors and had to keep their eyes open while the blinding light fried their retinas.

MATT: I have heard you are a religious woman. Is that true?

COLEEN: I'm not a religious woman; I am a Christian. I am a sinner saved by grace. I know where I am going, which is a big relief.

MATT: Well, hopefully not for a long time.

COLEEN: I don't mind, anytime. I even have a little song I sing. (Coleen sings). "Marching to the grave. Marching to the grave. We will sing rejoicing, marching to the grave."

MATT: That's two songs out of Coleen Gray today.

COLEEN: Well you missed one. (Coleen sings briefly). "Oh we ought to bake, a sunshine cake." That's from

Coleen today.

Riding High with Bing Crosby, and I did my own singing it that.

MATT: How is life today?

COLEEN: I have no complaints. Every day is enjoyable. I'm simplifying life. My husband and I, over the last thirty years, have had a great life. I'm blessed to have the world's greatest husband.

MATT: That is wonderful, Coleen. Thank you so much for this interview. It has been a big honor.

COLEEN: Take care, Matt. Bye.

Chapter Six:
KATHLEEN HUGHES

Kathleen Hughes is best known for her work at Universal Studios. She appeared in the Science Fiction classic, *It Came from Outer Space*, and the camp classic, *Cult of the Cobra*. She has also appeared in the films *The Glass Web, For Men Only*, and many others. Kathleen is married to former movie producer Stanley Rubin and lives in Los Angeles. Below is our interview from October 22, 2009.

MATT: Can you tell me where you are from, Kathleen?

KATHLEEN: I was born in the Hollywood hospital in Hollywood. I have lived in Hollywood my entire life except for a year in London. I have lived within the same three-mile radius my entire life.

MATT: Really?

KATHLEEN: Yes. I think that's very unusual.

MATT: Me too. Is there any reason?

KATHLEEN: Well, there was no reason to go anywhere else.

MATT: What were you like as a young child growing up here in Hollywood?

KATHLEEN: Oh God! (Laughs). I was just awful. I was a creep.

Nobody liked me. Kids made fun of me. I would walk down my street and boys would beat me up. It was no fun growing up. I just felt ugly and I felt like I had a pointy head. I wore sensible shoes, which made people make fun of me. I had braces on my teeth for four years. And I was very tall.

MATT: How tall?

KATHLEEN: (Kathleen makes a sad face and goes into a young girl's voice) I got to be five-foot nine inches, and now I'm only five-foot, six inches. I'd like to be five-foot, nine inches again.

MATT: Being tall is overrated. I am six-foot, three inches, and I bang my head all the time.

KATHLEEN: (Laughs). Oh yes!

MATT: Did you know growing up you wanted to be an actress?

KATHLEEN: Yes. Very early on, I knew. My uncle lived a few blocks away. My uncle was F. Hugh Herbert, the screenwriter and playwright. I spent a lot of time at his house because my two cousins were like sisters, and I was over there all the time. My uncle always had directors there, and I would listen to them talk, and it sounded very exciting, and he would take us on to sets of movies that he was making, and that was very exciting to me, and I thought, *Gee, I would like to do that.*

MATT: Did he have any famous people over? Did you ever get star struck?

KATHLEEN: Well, nobody that was really special. I remember Patsy Kelly. One of the movies was like *Hit Parade of 1930 Something?* I don't remember the people much. I just remember it looked like a lot of fun. Oh, but he was friends with Frank Morgan, and we used to go over to Frank Morgan's house in the summer and swim in his pool, and sometimes, Frank would swim with us. That was exciting.

MATT: How did you get your start in the business?

KATHLEEN: After I graduated from Fairfax High, I went to Los Angeles City College, and I read in the paper about a scholarship contest for a little theater called the Gellar Workshop. I entered the contest. All you had to do was send in your picture. I sent in my picture and I won a scholarship. After the first year, they gave me a second scholarship. During my second scholarship, I was appearing in a play one night called *Night Over Taos* by Maxwell Anderson. There was a talent scout from Fox studios in the audience, and I was sort of young and gorgeous, at that point. After the show, he suggested that I come out to Fox and test. My uncle was under contract to Fox, though he had nothing to do with my being discovered. My uncle said to me, "I will make the test for you," and he made the best test possible! It's called a "personality test." It was not a scene; it was a test in which he spoke to me. It was very clever, and it ended up with me blowing kisses at something that you couldn't tell what it was. Finally, I turned it around and it was a picture of Darryl F. Zanuck, the head of Fox studios. That went over BIG with Mr. Zanuck. I ended up with a seven-year contract that lasted three years. It was around fourteen films.

MATT: Which movie was first?

KATHLEEN: *Roadhouse* with Cornel Wilde. That was my first

A glamour shot of Kathleen.

picture. I loved every minute of it. There are lots of scenes of me.

MATT: Sadly, we recently lost Richard Widmark. What was he like?

KATHLEEN: Very friendly. I liked him a lot. One day after we finished the movie, I was walking along Beverly

Boulevard with a friend of mine, and this was before I had changed my name. My name then was Betty. So, I was walking along with my friend and we passed along Richard Widmark. He said, "Oh, hello Betty." Well, my friend just freaked. "That's Richard Widmark!! He knows your name!" He was a very nice man. They all were. Celeste Holm was very sweet to me.

MATT: Around this time, didn't you lose out on a role to Marilyn Monroe?

KATHLEEN: Yes. She got my part in something. Shortly after I signed at Fox, I got a call from casting, and they asked, "Can you dance?" I said, "I don't know. I never tried." I wanted to take dance lessons when I was young, but I never got them. I saw the Meglin Kiddies, if anyone even remembers them. I think Shirley Temple was a Meglin Kiddie. I adored them. Anyway, the studio agent said, "Go to stage 9 tomorrow morning and you will meet a dance director and we will see." Well, this poor, patient dance director—from nine in the morning till six at night—he tried to teach me one simple time step, really simple. I couldn't get it. My feet were not connected to my brain. He was so patient and so nice, but I couldn't connect. I think one reason was that I was terrified that if I got the part, I would have to fly to the location. I had never flown before, and I didn't want to! Maybe that's why there was a disconnection. I just couldn't learn it. The studio said, "Forget it. We will get some-body else." Marilyn had been under contract and was dropped just when I was signed. I had seen her perform. She was in a show that Fox studio club put on at the beginning of the year, and she sang and danced in it. She was fabulous! So I guess the studio knew how great she was. Here's the thing:

they had wanted to use four contract players to play four dancing girls, but there were only three contract players that looked right for the part, or where available. So, they said, "Well, let's get Marilyn back. She can do it." And so, Marilyn came back and did it. And it was great, of course. Marilyn danced beautifully. I eventually started taking dance lessons, and I can dance now. I can pick up a step in thirty seconds.

MATT: There's always *Dancing with the Stars*.

KATHLEEN: (Laughs). I don't think so.

MATT: After Fox, you worked with Universal for some time. How did that happen?

KATHLEEN: What happened was, after I left Fox, I did a lot of freelancing. I did TV, and live TV, which was really terrifying. One of the live shows I did was over at CBS. It was *The Frank Sinatra Show*. I got to work with Frank Sinatra, who did not like me at all. I was invisible to him. When I met him years later, he said, "Pleased to meet ya," and he turned around and left. I do not know why, but he did not like me. I was in a skit with him and Leo Durocher. I was playing a sexy nurse in a psychiatrist's office, just the three of us. A good friend of Sinatra's, Don McGuire, was in the audience to watch the dress rehearsal, and he was under contract to Universal. He came backstage, and said to me, "You should be at Universal." This was only nine months after I left Fox. He said, "Do you have any footage? Do you have any film?" I had just finished a wonderful film called *For Men Only*. Now it's called *The Tall Lie* with Paul Henreid and Sally Field's mother, Margaret Field. I played a sexy college girl trying to seduce

Kathleen with Frank Sinatra.

Paul Henreid's character. It was a wonderful part, and so Universal ran it and signed me instantly. That was very nice.

MATT: How did you get involved with *It Came from Outer Space*?

KATHLEEN: Wait a minute, that's an interesting story. I believe I was already, no I couldn't have been yet. Around that time, I became Miss 3D of 1953, because I was so three dimensional Universal wanted to test the 3D cameras on me, so they asked me if I would mind being in this camera test. I said, "Sure." I was wearing a bathing suit, and there was a long runway, and they just had me walking back and forth on this runway to test the cameras. I asked about the picture, and I said, "Is there a part in it for me?" Well, Barbara Rush was the female star, and I said, "What else is there?" They said, "There is a much too tiny part. It's too small for you. You just finished a second lead." I said, "It's 3D. I want to be in it." I just kept after them, and finally, they said, "Okay, all right, you can have it!"

MATT: You were very tenacious.

KATHLEEN: Yes. I thought that would be a good career move. Nobody else at the time was helping me with my career. My agents didn't do ANYTHING.

MATT: Was that the first 3D movie?

KATHLEEN: No. To my knowledge, the first 3D movie was called *Bwana Devil*. There were quite a few before *It Came from Outer Space*. Then, Universal decided to make another 3D picture in which I starred, called *The Glass Web* with Edward G. Robinson. If it ever played in 3D, it only played for a week. It basically ran flat. At some movie festivals, they run it in 3D, and I just love it. They have had at least two or three 3D festivals at the Egyptian Theatre in Hollywood.

MATT: Did Ray Bradbury have much to do with the movie?

Kathleen showing how 3D she can be!

KATHLEEN: Not much, I don't think so. I never met him during the movie. He wasn't around. I met him at the Egyptian Theatre a couple of times while we were interviewed together. I had him autograph a poster for me. It's hanging in my bathroom.

MATT: Were you familiar with any of the Universal horror movies?

KATHLEEN: I was familiar with *Phantom of the Opera* and what they called the Phantom stage. I was off and on the Phantom stage for various reasons. Sometimes, we would have class there, or rehearse. I was very familiar with that stage.

MATT: Where was *It Came from Outer Space* filmed?

KATHLEEN: I have no idea where the desert scenes were filmed. My stuff was done right there on the lot at Universal.

MATT: Since it was being shown in 3D, was there anything different about how you were filming the movie?

KATHLEEN: Slightly different. (Kathleen stands up to demonstrate as she speaks). You had to be aware that anything that sticks out toward the audience was going to really stick out. So, you know, if I was standing this way (Kathleen stands facing me) and you were the camera, it would pretty much be flat. If I stood like this (Kathleen stands on an angle flexing her arm) my elbow would be out to the twelfth row.

MATT: What did you think when you saw yourself on the big screen in 3D?

KATHLEEN: I loved it and the reaction that I get today when I go to a festival and they run it. There is this murmur that goes through the audience when my scene comes on. I love it. I just love it.

MATT: Do you believe in aliens?

KATHLEEN: I don't really think about it. Anything's possible. I really don't spend a lot of time wondering about it.

MATT: Soon after, you did *Cult of the Cobra.* Did you audition for that movie?

KATHLEEN: I didn't have to audition for anything when I was under contract. They told me what I was going to be in. I never complained; I never argued. They would say, "You are going to be in this picture." My response was always, "Okay, fine, give me the script." But *Cult* was a very unpleasant situation. The director hated me and I hated the director. He used to give me direction in a loud, clear voice in front of the entire stage. He would say things like, "Don't be so coy, Kathleen!" Well, that's something he could have whispered in my ear. I didn't like him, but I loved working in movies, and I didn't care. I just wanted to work.

MATT: Is there more to why it was so unpleasant?

KATHLEEN: I got the flu while I was working on that movie. I got the intestinal flu, and when you have that, you don't know what you are going to have to do first—both ends are going. I had to stay home, obviously. I couldn't possibly be at the studio, and as a result, they treated me so badly. There are records of this. There is a person in New York who has all this stuff. I can't think of his name. He is well-known in film collecting. Anyway, I was telling him once about how they blamed me for production delays. When I came back after being sick, I walked past the assistant director's desk and just happened to glance down at some papers, and the paper said it was my fault and that I had delayed production. The whole thing, as I said, was unpleasant. I couldn't work with the flu. What can I tell you? That was the least pleasant experience I had on a film.

MATT: When did your association with Universal end?

KATHLEEN: I was there for three years. *Cult of the Cobra* was my last picture for them. I got married to Stanley (film producer Stanley Rubin), who was under contract at the studio, and I think they felt that once I got married I was useless to them for publicity. I didn't care. I was doing movies to kill time till I found a husband. (Laughs).

MATT: Can you tell me more about meeting your husband,

Kathleen at her Los Angeles home in 2009.
Photo by Matt Beckoff.

producer Stanley Rubin? I know you have been together for a very long time.

KATHLEEN: Universal had sent me to the Mar Del Plata Film Festival in Argentina. They sent a whole bunch of us from the studio. This was a huge film festival with delegations from all over the world. I became friendly with the French delegation and the Russian delegation, and had such a good time. Well, the very last day before we came home, they had a picnic for us. I ate something that I guess nobody else ate. I got the worst food poisoning of my life. It was so bad that I lost ten pounds in one week. I got back to the States the next day, and I thought, *I can't go into the studio.* So, I decided I would go to Palm Springs and lie in the sun.

Something I would never do again. I was sitting on the edge of the pool and a girl came along and started talking and we were asking each other where the other was from and, you know, so and so. She then said, "Do you know Stanley Rubin?" Well, he had been phoning me and asking me out, and I had been turning him down. He had been asking me out for months, but I wasn't interested. I saw him linked with all kinds of movie stars and starlets. When I told her I was not interested, she said, "You're crazy. This is the nicest man I have ever met." I said, "Wow, really? Well if you run into him tell him to call me again." So, she did, and he called, and he said, "How would you like to go out to dinner and then we can go over to Fox and we can see a print of *River of No Return* with Marilyn Monroe." I said, "That sounds wonderful." I forgot to tell you, I had met Stanley at a party once. I was dating a very handsome actor named Lance Fuller, and Lance knew everybody. Lance was under contract to Universal, at the time. Lance took me to a party, and then he saw Stanley and he brought me over to introduce him. He said, "This is Stanley Rubin." I said, "How do you do?" and I turned around to see if there was anyone exciting in the room (laughs). I had no idea. That was when he started calling me and I kept turning him down. I just didn't think he was for me. So, that night, when he came to pick me up for our date to go to dinner and the movie, it was like I had never seen him before. I opened the front door to my apartment, and it was like I had been hit with lightning. It was the most amazing reaction, and if he had said, "I changed my mind, let's just go get married instead of going to dinner," I would have said "Yes." Two months later, we were engaged, and two weeks after that, we were married at my Uncle F. Hugh Herbert's house.

MATT: How long have you been married now?

KATHLEEN: It's been over fifty-five years.

MATT: That is remarkable. Thank you, Kathleen; this has been a lot of fun.

KATHLEEN: You're so welcome.

Chapter Seven:
JUDITH O'DEA

Universal Studios has introduced about every screen monster one could think. Many of them have become pop culture icons, such as Dracula, Frankenstein's Monster, the Mummy, and the Wolf Man.

In 1968, the movie *Night of the Living Dead* definitely put the "Zzzzz's" in Zombies. Yes, Zombies were featured on the big screen in past productions dating back to the 1930s. However, it wasn't until they started *coming for Barbra* when zombies joined forces and became part of our pop culture, as well. Actress Judith O'Dea made her screen debut when she played Barbra in the classic movie *Night of the Living Dead*. She later pursued other endeavors and returned to show business sporadically. Within the last few years, Judith O'Dea has resumed acting and is busier than ever! She took time for the following interview.

MATT: *Night of the Living Dead* was your first movie role. How did your involvement with the film come about?

JUDITH: Years before *Night of the Living Dead* was even a glimmer in the minds of George Romero and Company, I had worked with Karl Hardman, Marilyn Eastman, and Chuck Craig recording commercials at Hardman Associates. We all had great times together. Then, I moved to Hollywood, California, hoping to make it big in the movies. Almost a year later, I received a call from Karl

Judith fights off a zombie.

asking me if I'd like to come back home to audition for a film he and Marilyn were going to make with George Romero, Russ Streiner, and Jack Russo. Without hesitation, I hopped on a plane, flew back to Pittsburgh, and auditioned for the film. I'm so glad I did. Getting the role of "Barbra" changed my life.

MATT: In one scene, your character, Barbra, runs into a gas pump. Is it true that you nearly knocked it over during filming because you used too much force?

JUDITH: Yes, that's right. I plowed right into the pump. The fact that it was not securely bolted down was the reason it almost toppled on George.

MATT: I read that originally Barbra was supposed to make it out of the house alive. Why did George Romero decide to change your character's fate?

JUDITH: That's a question better suited for George, Matt. I really don't know the answer. But I'm glad he went with the change. It made for a better ending. Don't you think?

MATT: Yes. Also, wasn't Barbra's character originally supposed to be a much stronger woman? And that once filming started, it was decided the "terrified Barbara" would better suit the movie?

JUDITH: Here again, I really don't know the answer to that question, Matt. But I do believe George's decision to allow me to play "Barbra" terrified was a good one. It seems more honest to me. Here is a person who has just seen her brother killed and is running for her life from something she doesn't understand at all. Being terrified and confused seems an appropriate response to a horrific situation.

MATT: I don't know if you would know the answer to this, but do you know how many actors were hired to portray the zombies?

JUDITH: You've got me there. I have no idea. I bet Russ Streiner or Jack Russo would know though.

MATT: What was your first reaction to seeing the actors made up to look like the zombies? Is it true they used Bosco chocolate sauce as blood?

JUDITH: I thought the zombie make-up was great, especially knowing what a limited budget we had to do it. And yes, I believe we used either Bosco or Hershey chocolate sauce for blood. It filmed incredibly realistically.

MATT: Is it true that the first scene was actually the last scene shot? Was there any reason this was done?

JUDITH: I can't say for sure. But I think you are right. Why it was done this way might have been for a variety of reasons, location and cast availability, budget concerns, more expeditious, etc. This often happens in filmmaking.

MATT: At a time when movies were being made in color, why was it decided to film it in black and white?

JUDITH: My best guess is that budget had everything to do with it. Shooting in color is far more expensive. Our budget was tiny, so shooting in black and white gave us more bang for the buck, so to speak. And here again, in hindsight, it was a great decision, wasn't it? I think the movie looks far, far better in black and white than in color. It adds to the frightening mood.

MATT: The somewhat violent and sudden ending was shocking. What did you think about the ending when you read it in the script?

JUDITH: I can't say I got the opportunity to read it in the script. For the most part, George just told me what he wanted me to do before shooting each scene. As I recall, much of the dialogue was ad lib.

MATT: Being it was your first film, was there any worry on your part that you would lose out on work because of a film like this?

JUDITH: I never even gave that a thought. It was just so exciting making the film. I never once imagined it could have a negative impact on my career.

MATT: Duane Jones, who starred as Ben, was one of the first African-American men to have a lead role in a horror movie. Do you remember any talk of this around the time of filming?

JUDITH: No, I don't recall any such talk. We all were just focused on what we had to do in the very limited time we had to do it. If such things were talked about, most probably, they were talked about among George, Russ, Jack, Karl, and Marilyn.

MATT: Can you share a story about working with the late Duane Jones?

JUDITH: One that comes to mind is our scene in the kitchen hammering boards across the door. Pounding nails didn't come easily for Duane, so we eventually had the nails already sunk half way before shooting. But if you'd given Duane a book or a good play, he'd be all over it. That was really his element.

MATT: What is George A. Romero like as a director? Did you enjoy working for him?

JUDITH: George is an extremely talented and creative director. I thoroughly enjoyed working with him. He knows

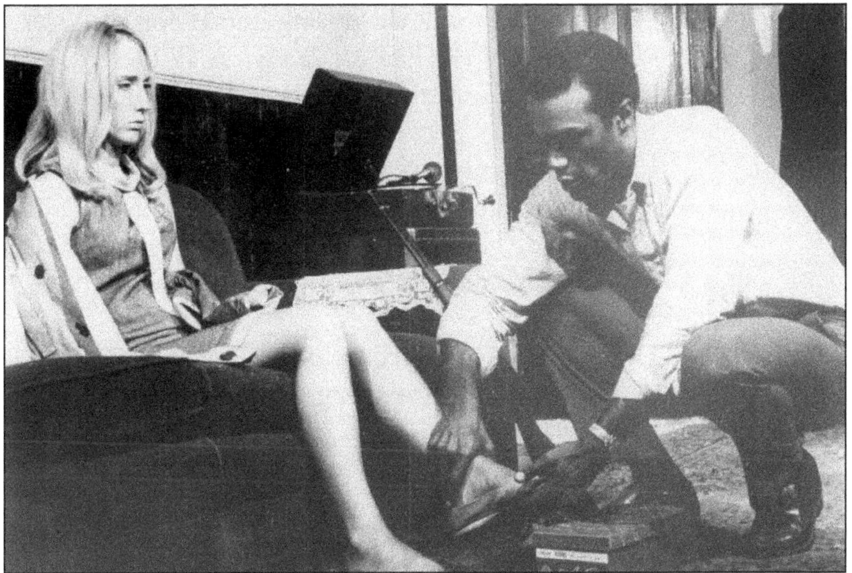

Judith and Duane Jones in a scene from *Night of the Living Dead*.

what he wants, and is willing to allow the actor the freedom to produce it in his or her own way. And if that doesn't work, he'll help you find the best way to achieve those results.

MATT: How was the film received when it first opened?

JUDITH: I think it shocked the viewing public and critics alike. No other film before it was as immediately graphic. Nor did those earlier films have all their major characters end up dead by film's end. It was also break-through in that an intelligent Black man was cast in the lead to fight for survival with a white woman.

MATT: Have you seen any of the sequels? If so, what did you think of them?

JUDITH: Yes, I have seen *some* of the sequels, but not all. To be honest, that genre is not quite my cup of tea, so to speak. But please don't hold that against me.

MATT: What do you think the lasting impression of *Night of the Living Dead* had on audiences all these years later? It's been over forty years as of this interview.

JUDITH: I am continually awed, humbled, and extremely grateful. Without a doubt, having been so fortunate to be involved in the making of this film has influenced my life in an extraordinary way.

MATT: Did you have any inclination having appeared in the movie that it was going to be a groundbreaking film?

JUDITH: None whatsoever!

MATT: What did you do after *Night of the Living Dead*?

JUDITH: For the last forty-plus years, I have been working on stage in California and making several more films. In fact, I've been busier in film these past five years than ever before. In addition, I've had a second wonderfully fulfilling career as a teacher of oral presentations for major corporations throughout the United States.

MATT: Do you enjoy doing autograph conventions? What is something you usually hear during the weekend from your fans?

JUDITH: Yes, I love going to the autograph conventions. It gives me a wonderful opportunity to thank so many fans for supporting *Night of the Living Dead* all these years. The question I am asked most is "did any of us know that *Night* would become such a classic?"

MATT: "Scream Queens" usually have hardcore devoted fans. Would you say so?

Judith today.

JUDITH: I think you're right, and I'm sure happy for that.

MATT: You said you have been working lately on some movies. Can we expect to see more of Judith O'Dea?

JUDITH: Absolutely! The old girl isn't down yet.

MATT: What are some upcoming projects you are working on?

JUDITH: There are two films in the works. I won't jinx the process by naming them. I've also written and am directing and performing in a radio drama for "Sun Sounds of Arizona."

MATT: Is there a place on the web where fans can keep up to date with your upcoming projects?

JUDITH: There are two sites fans can check out: www.damesofthedead.com and www.odeacommunications.com.

Chapter Eight:
KAREN BLACK

Karen Black is a dynamo. She is an actress, playwright, singer, and songwriter. For her work on the silver screen, she received an Academy Award nomination. She has also won two Golden Globe Awards for her work in *Five Easy Pieces* and *The Great Gatsby*. For her musical contributions to the film *Nashville*, in which she also co-starred, Karen was nominated for music's highest honor, the Grammy. She is also an award-winning stage performer having begun her career as an actress on the New York stage. Karen Black insists that she has never appeared in horror films. She refers to them as "Sci-Fi movies." I will leave the reader to decide that one. I won't debate her. I will say, however, that some of Karen's movies have scared the hell out of me.

Karen worked with genre icon Dan Curtis on the film *Burnt Offerings*, as well as the legendary television movie *Trilogy of Terror* in which Karen played four different roles. She also worked with the Master of Suspense, Alfred Hitchcock, on his very last film, *Family Plot*. She is also known for her role in the action film *Airport 1975*. Since then, Karen has appeared in many horror and science-fiction films including *Killer Fish*, a remake of *Invaders from Mars* directed by Tobe Hooper, and one of the *Children of the Corn* movies. Since the beginning of the 21st century, Karen has garnered a whole new crop of horror fans with her work in the cult Rob Zombie movie *House of 1,000 Corpses*. For these and many more movies, Karen has certainly left her mark on the genre, and whether she likes it or not, she is one of the best loved "Scream Queens" of her generation.

MATT: Karen, can you tell me how you got your start in show business?

KAREN: I went to New York City and got an apartment in Coldwater Flats with lots of windows. It was very hot; it's kind of tropical in New York City, the weather in the summer. I had big windows and I could pull the shade down and be naked so I could be cool. Then, I could get dressed and pull the shade up with the lights on or put the lights off if I wanted to be naked, but then I couldn't see anything and that was kind of a problem. I got little jobs and lied about my age. I would say I was older to get hired. I worked in a hotel, where all I did was hear people complain about the hotel. I was probably earning about $30 to $50 a week. I ate a lot of brown rice and Lorna Doone cookies. I got *Backstage* magazine and I would go for every single thing in it, all the dancing, singing, and acting parts, and I would do that all day, every day. I would get Off-Broadway shows, and after four years, I got a Broadway show.

MATT: Do you remember the title of that show?

KAREN: Well, of course: I was nominated for the Drama Critics' Circle Award for it. It was *The Playroom*. As a result, I was asked to meet Francis Ford Coppola and that was the beginning of my film career. Mr. Coppola's first movie was actually his college master's thesis and was called *You're a Big Boy Now*, and it was really quite something. Soon after that, I went to L.A. and started doing movies. I did a lot of television and then movies.

MATT: Would you say that *Nashville* was one of your first big movie roles?

KAREN: No, it was in the cluster of films I did when I first started out. When I went to Los Angeles, I had Francis Coppola's picture, *You're a Big Boy Now*, soon coming out. I had Kevin Castleman as my agent. He flew in to see me, when I was in New York doing *The Playroom* and signed me immediately. I would fly to L.A. and Kevin Castleman would pick me up in his car, since I was not driving at the time, and he would take me to all these things. Then, I met Dennis (Hopper) and Peter (Fonda) and they auditioned me for *Easy Rider*, which was a wonderful time because Dennis was improvising and he was very brilliant and very dynamic. Then, I auditioned with a lot of people for *Five Easy Pieces* and I got the part.

MATT: How did you enjoy working with your co-star Jack Nicholson in *Five Easy Pieces*?

KAREN: I loved him. I love him. He is a very great spirit, a very, very great spirit, very present, very real, and very accessible. He is a very friendly, congenial man. He is very great and has perfect integrity as an artist and will not do anything but his best at every moment. He is a great, great person.

MATT: One of my favorite films that you did was *Family Plot*. Wasn't that Alfred Hitchcock's last film?

KAREN: Right.

MATT: It was originally supposed to be called *Deceit*.

KAREN: *Deceit*, no, I don't remember that. I do remember that he didn't know what to call it. I don't think they even decided while we were shooting. I think he and Ernest Lehman did not have a great time

Rare, on-set photo of Karen with Alfred Hitchcock during the filming of *Family Plot*.

writing that movie. It was really hard and stressful. I think that may have been part of the reason Hitchcock had a heart monitor put in. I have some vague remembrance of something like that.

MATT: You originally auditioned for the role of Blanche, or you originally wanted the role of Blanche, correct? I am not sure if you auditioned for it or not.

KAREN: I never auditioned for it. I could never get a message to Mr. Hitchcock. I wanted the role of Blanche. I loved the role, I had an accent I was going to do and I would have been hilariously funny. I told my strange manager, who was not even in show business, and I don't think Hitchcock ever got the message. Then at the beginning of shooting, I confessed to Mr. Hitchcock that I really had wanted to play Blanche, and he said (Karen goes into her Hitchcock voice), "Oh, no, much too low-brow for you, dear." That's a quote! I think he had just never seen *Five Easy Pieces*. I'm sure he hadn't.

MATT: Wasn't there a funny costume story?

KAREN: Yes. When I met Mr. Hitchcock in his office, he was with Edith Head, who was doing the wardrobe. I walked up to Mr. Hitchcock to tell him with warmth and grace how delighted I was to be in the cast. He looked a little bit stunned at what I was wearing. In those days, it was the 1970s, and you wore layers. I had a silk blouse, over which was a long sleeve jacket. I had on a big leather belt, pants, those funny stacked heels, jewelry, and a big leather hat. I said to him "Oh no, this is not what I am wearing in your movie!" to which he replied (Karen dons her Hitchcock voice once again) "No, you can wear that. We'll just have to write in a nightmare sequence!"

MATT: Wasn't Roy Thinnes originally hired to play Adamson in the movie, but that soon after filming began, Alfred Hitchcock fired him? Did you have to reshoot any scenes?

KAREN: The truth is that Mr. Hitchcock said that Mr. Thinnes didn't seem to be an evil person. Here is the quote I remember, something like, "He is not the kind of person who would be capable of committing these crimes. He doesn't seem to be an evil person." That is what it was and Mr. Hitchcock would fire people. He told me I had to be less lovable; the audience should not have "that much compassion for my character." He also told me I needed to have a mid-Atlantic accent; the Illinois accent had to go. He was very shrewd and he had to have a picture right. The first shot in the movie is very, very complicated, and the first guy that was doing it wasn't getting it right. I don't know if it was the cinematographer or the camera operator. I honestly don't know who, but Mr. Hitchcock fired him and hired someone else the very next day. He had to have it right, that was it. By the way, I don't know how long Roy Thinnes was involved with the movie. And I don't remember reshooting anything. We may have and I forgot, I just don't remember.

MATT: Was it an overall pleasant experience working for Mr. Hitchcock?

KAREN: I loved it, it was great. He was so lovable, so avuncular. He would sit and tell us limericks when we were together. He was just great and he would always try to catch me on my vocabulary. He would try to use words that would force you to say, "I don't know what that means," but I never did because I always caught him. He would say (Karen dons her Hitchcock voice) "You are very perspicacious today," and I would say, "You mean keenly perceptive." And he would say "Yes, keenly perceptive, quite right." He loved to have fun; he was a fun-loving guy.

MATT: What a great honor it must have been to work with him.

KAREN: Yes, it was a great honor.

MATT: Soon after, or around the time of *Family Plot* you did a television movie called *Trilogy of Terror*, and I read that, originally, you did not want to do it, but you were persuaded to do it?

KAREN: At the same time *Trilogy* came about, there was a

television movie that was offered to me in which I would have played a whore. It was a great role and a wonderful show, and I didn't do it. My problem at that time was nobody told me what was a good idea and what wasn't and I sure didn't know. Jill Clayburgh got the part and it made her career and that's how she started. Meanwhile, I do *Trilogy of Terror*, which started me into a horror genre, which has nothing to do with my spirit or my talent, nothing to do with it. Who wanted me to do it? It was my manager, again the same fellow who had nothing to do with show business. He plopped himself down in the middle of my lovely living room until four in the morning trying to convince me to take the movie. At the time I was married to a guy, an actor, named Robert Burton. I said, "Okay. I'll do it if Skipper (Robert's nickname) can play the student in the *Julie* segment." My manager called Dan Curtis, and Dan said, "Sure, have Skipper play her student."

MATT: Weren't you also attracted to playing one of the female characters?

KAREN: I was attracted to the story with the sexy twin sister and the virgin spinster.

MATT: Oh, yes, Millicent and Therese.

KAREN: Millicent yes, I thought it would be a good while before I got to play a Millicent character and I liked that opportunity.

MATT: The differences between Millicent and Therese were a mile apart.

KAREN: She was a hot number, that Therese. She was walking around absolutely ready.

Karen in the television movie *Trilogy of Terror*.

MATT: Did you enjoy wearing the sexy attire and the
            blonde wig?

KAREN: Well, I was a real sexy girl, so yeah I liked it. It was
            good fun.

MATT: I have read that you were very into dressing up
            your characters and providing your own costumes
            and ideas about their characteristics. Is that true?

KAREN: It depends, you know. Sure, I like to look like the
            character I think I am playing. I don't remember
            doing costumes for *Trilogy*, so I don't know who
            told you about that. I don't have a memory of it. I
            do know when I worked with the genius, Ivan Passer,
            and we did *Born to Win*, I had my own cats in that
            movie. I brought them to New York. One of those
            cats' back legs didn't work because it had had cat
            pneumonia, or whatever. The cat should be dead,

but I nursed it back to life basically with grape juice. In case anyone wants to know, just squirt grape juice into these cat's mouths that are ill. He lived and the doctor was shocked! Anyway, in *Born to Win*, I did a lot of stuff. But ordinarily, I mean, of course, I am going to want to look like the character.

MATT: What sticks out for me in that movie is the last shot of you crouching down twirling that butcher knife with that huge grin and those sharp teeth and the crazy look on your face. Wasn't it your idea to get those teeth made?

KAREN: Yeah, Dan thought that was pretty silly of me, but I said, "I think she should have teeth like the doll has." So, he had them made, but he really didn't think it was a good idea. Then, of course, when he saw them, and I also did my own makeup to look like the doll, you know, a little bit of shadows and darkness under the eyes and so forth. After I created that look, then he saw that it was a really good idea.

MATT: The teeth seem to have stuck in everyone's mind after all these years. Do you regret suggesting it?

KAREN: No, I'm just not selling that picture any more when I do autograph conventions.

MATT: What was Dan Curtis like as a director?

KAREN: Dan had his own way of shooting. He uses a lot of little angles. I think when we did *Trilogy*, he let me write things, he let me change the conversation with my mother. The first conversation I had with her, because you need to know that she is a really suppressive person. I changed the dialogue so that you could tell that.

MATT: I also read that there were scenes that were cut from the film?

KAREN: Yes, I was trying to get out of a window, or something. It was just so scary, so much scarier than what you've ever seen. I was locked in and I couldn't open the door and things would break. Yeah, there were scenes cut, it was too horrible, and it would have been even scarier.

MATT: Your next project with Dan Curtis was *Burnt Offerings*. Did you know that he specifically wanted you for the role of Marian in *Burnt Offerings*?

KAREN: I think I was in San Francisco doing *Family Plot*. I remember having a Winnebago, and he came up and asked me almost on bended knee to do *Burnt Offerings*, and I told him, "You know, I'm pregnant." He said, "I want you to do this movie." So, I did. I am glad I did it. I'm glad I knew him.

MATT: Yes, *Burnt Offerings* and *Family Plot* were both in 1976.

KAREN: Yeah, they came out then, but I was pregnant in 1975 when we filmed *Burnt Offerings*.

MATT: It is hard to tell that you were pregnant in the movie. You pulled it off great.

KAREN: I have a very long waist. I didn't show for a long time because I had these stupid doctors who told me to eat very little. Finally, when I was seven months pregnant, I went to my chosen doctor, who was going to deliver the baby, and he said, "You better eat, because your baby is four pounds, and if you don't eat more, you are not going to have a natural delivery." I ate my heart out, and Hunter was born more than seven pounds, and I had a natural delivery, and a very, very good child birth, the day after Christmas.

MATT: I know that Oliver Reed, when you were in the pool scene together, he kept shifting you around so that he would get more camera time. Do you remember?

KAREN: He was a terrific actor, but he had really started out as an extra, and so he was always worried about being seen. He would say to Dan Curtis (as she goes into her Oliver Reed voice) "Dan, Dan, lovely idea, a really lovely idea. I am just so concerned about her health and sickness that I'll rush over here and sit on this chair and hold her hand here," and, of course, he is going all the way around with his face on camera. Everyone has their thing. I worry about my eyes looking nice. Someone said to me yesterday, "You are not just another pretty face," and I said, "I would really love to be a pretty face."

MATT: One of my favorite things about *Burnt Offerings* is in the movie you worked with two of my favorite actresses, Eileen Heckart and Bette Davis. First, I would like to ask what it was like to work with Eileen Heckart?

KAREN: She was so good that I nearly fell over backwards, she was that good. The only other person that happened with was Tilda Swinton.

MATT: *Burnt Offerings* was one of Bette Davis's final pictures. What was it like working with her?

KAREN: She was a very magnetic performer. I do like to tell this one story. We were doing a scene in a greenhouse with flowers, like a patio greenhouse. And during a scene I said to myself, "I've lost my sense of character, my sense of place, my sense of story, what happened?" It turned out I was watching her act.

MATT: You were that captivated?

KAREN: Yeah. I was just being entertained by this woman, and I forgot what I was doing.

MATT: That's incredible. I've heard she has that effect on people. After you had done *Trilogy of Terror* and *Burnt Offerings* with Dan Curtis, your image somewhat changed. You had gone from doing dramatic movies to horror. Was there any regret?

KAREN: Dan Curtis has never done a horror movie.

MATT: I am sorry, Sci-Fi.

KAREN: It never crossed my mind, how would I be aware of that? I was just doing my job and I had just done *Five Easy Pieces* and *Easy Rider*, and those had nothing to do with scary movies. That scary movie thing is too bad that that happened.

MATT: You were nominated for a third Golden Globe Award for your performance in *The Day of the Locust*. That film also featured your *Burnt Offerings* co-star, Burgess Meredith. Did you enjoy doing that film?

KAREN: It was horrible, they treated me so horribly. It ruined my career. People started rumors about me. I was kind, I was never cruel to anybody, but people would start rumors about me. It ruined my career. I did love Burgess Meredith very dearly. One time, when his character was very sick in the movie I leaned over and held his hand and it was cold and clammy. He was mocking up with such veracity from himself that he was actually cold and clammy. He was great. I missed being nominated by five votes, for the Academy Award.

MATT: I heard that before.

KAREN: That darling is probably a story I have already told you. I was at a cocktail party once, and a man approached me and said, "I should not tell you this, but I am going to. I work for the place that does the polling for the Oscars, and the truth is you were five votes from being nominated. I've never seen anything like it before or since."

MATT: Why do you think you did not get the nomination?

KAREN: When I was doing a film on the lot at Universal, some young man, an amateur movie maker, climbed the walls of the studio and came to my room. He wanted me to do this little movie of his where I would be playing a man. I thought to myself, "That's interesting, I want to try that!" He and my manager signed all these documents that stated this movie was purely experimental and that it would never be seen in a movie theater. I was quite a star at the time. Well, sure enough, he put the movie in theaters. And it was not a good movie. I had marks on my face to try and make a beard. It was disgusting. So, he broke all these agreements, and he put it in theaters, and then we went to court with him, and he had to take the movie out of the theaters. Then he, or somebody, wrote articles in *Hollywood Reporter* about how mean I was, and how I hurt his career. Here he was just using me to get ahead. It was kind of a degraded effort on his part trying to succeed in show business in some strange way.

MATT: That is terrible.

KAREN: The other reason was: I was asked to go on *The Tonight Show* very soon after I had Hunter. My mother and father were staying with me at the time to help. Of course, they were no help. I would have been great on the show and that would have been it. I would have been nominated, I am sure of it. My father thought I had better not go on it, fearing it was too soon after the birth. It was just days since I had given birth. I thought I was healthy enough, but, I did not go. That was a bad decision and I think that is how I lost that.

MATT: One movie that certainly sticks out in people's minds is *Airport 1975*. Did you film in an actual plane?

KAREN: It really was like a plane. I was shocked that it was a real fuselage, well I don't know if it was a "real" fuselage, but it was exactly the same mock-up. It was exactly the same size and everything just like the real thing even with the controls in the exact location.

MATT: Did you ever see the *Family Guy* episode where they spoofed you and the movie?

KAREN: I did. It was cute. My daughter said that they really didn't make too much fun of me, because they really can be scathing. They didn't treat me too badly so that was good.

MATT: As someone who enjoys a good conspiracy theory, I want to ask you about *Capricorn One*.

KAREN: I think I was working with Elliot Gould in that movie. Wonderful guy. I met him in The Chelsea

Hotel in New York City, long, long ago, before the movie. We were in the elevator together going up and it was the early 1970s, and I said, "You know, you look just like Elliot Gould." And he said, "That's funny, you look just like Karen Black." That is how we met.

MATT: Did you enjoy doing *Capricorn One*?

KAREN: My son, Hunter, was a little boy at the time, and I wouldn't leave him, so I think I upset people because I would be late on the set a little bit while I put him to sleep. He wasn't a child you could leave anywhere.

MATT: I would like to talk a bit more about the movie *Nashville*. I hope I am not confusing you.

KAREN: No, I remember my life.

MATT: Aside from being a talented actor, you are also an accomplished singer and songwriter. Didn't you contribute some songs to the movie, receiving a Grammy nomination for your efforts?

KAREN: Yes. I seem to remember writing some of those songs on some other set. When I met Robert Altman, I sang "Memphis" for him. I had already written "Memphis" for some other project. Robert said he was doing a movie in the coming fall with people who had to write their own country poems, and I said, "I write country songs and I'll sing you one." He said, "Well maybe you want to wait till later in the day and we'll have someone play the piano for you." It was at his office. I said, "No, I'll sing it now." He said "Maybe you want to bring your guitar tomorrow?" I said "No, I'll sing it now." I stood up by the fireplace in the office, and sang (Karen sings) "I'd like to go to Memphis, but I don't know the way. I'd like to tell you how I feel but I don't know what to say. I'd love to go to Heaven but I forgot how to pray." He said, "Welcome aboard."

MATT: Thank you for that little impromptu singing.

KAREN: We didn't have a contract for *Nashville*. It was just verbal and that happens all the time in Hollywood. People are always saying, every time I meet someone, "Well you know, it is so unlike people to be nice and sweet. It is so unlike people in Hollywood to be nice." I am like, "What the fuck are you talking about?" I am tired of this lousy generality because all the people I know are fabulous, beautiful people.

MATT: In that time period, I'm talking the 1970s, when you were at the height of your career, is there a personal favorite film of yours?

KAREN: The thing is, when you make a movie, you don't love the movie in a way but more so, the experience.

MATT: Is there a favorite experience that you had?

KAREN: Making *Five Easy Pieces* and *Gatsby* were incredibly happy, wonderful experiences, and *Nashville* as well, just ecstasy. I generally have a very happy experience making movies. Only a couple of movies have been *ridiculous*, and only three movies have been unhappy but we won't mention them.

MATT: As we mentioned a bit earlier, after films like *Trilogy of Terror* and *Burnt Offerings*, you were somewhat categorized as a horror movie actress. When you did *Come Back To The Five And Dime,*

Karen in 2009.
PHOTO BY MARYANN BATES.

Jimmy Dean, Jimmy Dean both on Broadway and on the big screen, I think it caught people's attention again and showed them what a dynamic, versatile actress you are. I think it lifted the "Scream Queen" label for a while. Do you think that makes any sense?

KAREN: Yes, I agree. You know, I would get reviews that said, "Best performance of the year." I worked very hard on the part. I worked for months on it. I did it on Broadway of course, and it was a very, very difficult role. I think I mastered it and I became a guy on the inside as well as on the outside, which was very hard. I think the gay guys thought that I had scoped them out or that I had really investigated all about them.

MATT: Not to jump nearly twenty years ahead in your career, but I know that you have to get off the phone soon. Before we get off, can we talk briefly about *House of 1,000 Corpses*, the Rob Zombie horror movie? Can you tell me how you got involved with it?

KAREN: I had a meeting with Rob, and after a few minutes, he said, "Okay, let's do it." Then, I just developed this character that was nuts and loving and very dedicated to her lifestyle. I thought it was a very honorable way to live.

MATT: And a nymphomaniac, wouldn't you say so?

KAREN: Definitely.

MATT: On the commentary, Rob Zombie said that you had a very big part in creating the look of your character, including the smoking of cigarettes. Is that something you do for your characters?

KAREN: I somehow knew I would have long blonde hair. I usually create everything about how a character looks, but I think the costumer and I wanted her to be in some sort of nightwear. They never shot my figure which was totally sublime at that moment. I don't know why, but they just never

Karen in the Rob Zombie movie *House of 1,000 Corpses*.

really shot my figure in the whole movie, too bad. Anyway, we shot all night, every night because he liked the nights. But he was most wonderful to work with, as he was encouraging and handsome.

MATT: *House of 1,000 Corpses* has now brought on a whole new generation of Karen Black fans. Would you agree?

KAREN: I agree with you and I find it to be true. Yesterday, and the day before at this autograph convention, I signed more *1,000 Corpses* pictures than from any other movie of mine.

MATT: Is there any reason why you didn't repeat the role of Mother Firefly in the sequel, *The Devil's Rejects*?

KAREN: Did you see it?

MATT: Yes I did, I saw both of them.

KAREN: Did that look like Mother Firefly to you?

MATT: No. I think Mother Firefly cared too much about her kids and in the second movie she sold them out.

KAREN: That was the first thing I said to Rob. I said, "You know, this is not the character I created." Mother Firefly would die for her children. No way would she let anyone hurt her children, she would jump in front of them and take the bullet. So, I felt that they hadn't cared and someone hadn't really noticed what I did. It was Rob's movie and he should have noticed who the character is and put her into the sequel. It was too small a part and they made a very bad deal financially, as well. For example, when we did *Easy Rider* and when we did *Five Easy*

Pieces, both started out as small budget projects. When the movies became big hits, the producers would call all the actors and cut them into the money as a way of saying "Thank You." *House of 1,000 Corpses* made $20 million alone on the DVD sales. So, for the sequel they said after we make $20 million, we will cut you in. Usually, a sequel doesn't make as much money as the first movie. I didn't know who they were trying to make a deal with but it wasn't me.

MATT: It wasn't the same without you. I know you have to go, Karen, so I will stop there. Thank you so much for doing this. I really appreciate it.

KAREN: It is my pleasure and it is a funny time of the month as there is so much happening.

Chapter Nine:
INGRID PITT

Ingrid Pitt is one of Britain's top "Scream Queens" and a regular star of the Hammer films, a whole subject in its own right. Some of Ingrid's horror movies include *The House That Dripped Blood, The Vampire Lovers, Countess Dracula,* and the heavily underrated *The Wicker Man.* She is also a talented writer, who has released several books. Each year, Ingrid Pitt fans from around the world reunite in England for an annual celebration hosted by Ingrid herself. She has a strong personality and is armed with a wicked sense of humor, as you will soon see.

MATT:	When you first started out acting, did you think you would become best known as a "Scream Queen"?
INGRID:	When I started out, I could see myself as another Dr. Fleming. Unfortunately, a little incident with rats at a lecture put me off from pursuing a medical career. Acting was only taken up because the alternative seemed to be secretarial work. No deep, driven ambition I'm afraid.
MATT:	One of your first screen appearances was a minor role in *A Funny Thing Happened on the Way to the Forum.* Do you like musical comedies?
INGRID:	I actually started acting with the Berlin Ensemble

in Berlin. I then went to America and did bits and pieces until I thought I had made the breakthrough with the Pasadena Playhouse. They were having a hard time and passing it on to me by not paying my wages. So, I passed into the "landlady in the lodgings," where I was staying by doing a moonlighting flit, selling my car and catching a plane to Spain. By chance, I stayed in a flat, where actors and newspapermen were staying and they inveigled me into the *Forum* film, as well as other work. I was very lucky.

MATT: How did your association with the Hammer films come about?

INGRID: I was at the premiere of *Alfred the Great*. At the party afterwards, I found myself sitting next to Hammer boss, James Carreras. We talked and it led to the parts in *Vampire Lovers* and *Countess Dracula*.

MATT: Did you have any trepidations about doing horror films at first? Did you want to be a different kind of actress?

INGRID: Not really. It was work, and as far as making films goes, one part is as good as another. It seemed like a good opportunity to put some caviar on the table, so I accepted it.

MATT: What did you first think when you read *The Vampires Lovers* script?

INGRID: I was sold on the idea before I even saw the script. I met up with the writer, Tudor Gates, for lunch at the Gay Hussar and he went through it with me. I thought it was great.

A publicity photo of Ingrid.

MATT: Did you have any issues with the nudity and lesbianism?

INGRID: The nudity, none. Lesbianism, well, I didn't even know that was what it was about until about six years ago, when it was being shown at the British Film Theatre on the Thames South Bank and it was advertised as a Lesbian oeuvre. Got me?

MATT: It looked like a lot of detail was put into the costumes and the set location. Where was the movie filmed?

INGRID: Mainly at Elstree Studios and in the Golf Club at Moor Park. And the costumes were great.

MATT: What was it like working with the great Peter Cushing?

INGRID: As anyone will tell you, Peter was very sweet. I told him one day that it was the anniversary of my father's birthday. When shooting was finished, he turned up with his wife Helen, and a big candle bedecked cake with "Happy Birthday to Ingrid's Dad" on it.

MATT: The next year, you starred in another vampire film, *Countess Dracula*. Is it true you replaced Diana Rigg, who turned the role down?

INGRID: I didn't know that, although I have heard that story. What I do know was that I was at the Theatre in Worthing watching a play when I heard in the interval, a couple of men discussing the new Hammer film. I thought they were talking about *Vampire Lovers*, so I chimed in. They were surprised when I told them I hadn't heard about *Countess Dracula*. Next morning, I rang Jimmy

Carreras. He told me that Peter Sasdy was casting and that I should speak to him. It was another trip to the Gay Hussar and I walked out a Countess.

MATT: The film was inspired by the real life story of Countess Elizabeth Bathory, a Hungarian countess accused of killing hundreds of virgin girls. Were you familiar with the history of it at all?

INGRID: Not at the time, I didn't. Later, I did do a trip to Romania along with Chris Lee. I was asked to sleep in a castle where the Countess used to rest her weary, blood-stained head after a heavy day in the dungeons. I was freezing my furbelows off, so I screamed, told the waiting press that I had seen the specter of the Countess, and we all sloped off to bed. I also read a book about the subject. I read the script and followed the instructions most of the time.

MATT: Why was your voice dubbed in *Countess Dracula*?

INGRID: I don't know. I had done *Where Eagles Dare* and several other English-speaking parts, as well as *Vampire Lovers*. The first I heard of it was when I received a bunch of flowers from the actress brought in to cover me. I went to see Jimmy and kicked up a fuss. He told me he would speak to [Peter] Sasdy immediately and have my voice restored. Later, he rang to say Sasdy had already destroyed the voice tracks. Bullshit, of course! However, there was nothing I could do about it. It was strange really because Sasdy had the heaviest Hungarian accent heard east of Budapest.

MATT: I read that you and director Peter Sasdy didn't get along well. Is there any truth to that?

INGRID: Take an educated guess.

MATT: You also appeared in the anthology film *The House That Dripped Blood*. Did you enjoy making that picture?

INGRID: It was different. I was originally up for one of the other parts, but I spoke to Jon Pertwee, who I had done *Dr. Who* with. He had already been cast in *The House That Dripped Blood*. He suggested I get the director Peter Duffell to give me the part of Carla, or whatever her name was. It was great, although Jon was a bit of a perfectionist. I'm happy it seems to have stood the test of time.

MATT: At one point in the segment, *The Cloak*, the character Paul Henderson says he misses the "old great horror movies," and mentions *Dracula*. He then adds, ". . . the one with Bela Lugosi of course, not this new fellow," clearly referring to Christopher Lee, who also appeared in the film. Were you aware of that? Or more importantly was Christopher Lee? Was that intentional?

INGRID: I don't think there was any intention of hiding the remark.

MATT: Speaking of Christopher Lee, you and he also appeared in one of my favorite movies, *The Wicker Man*. How did you get involved with the project?

INGRID: I read about it. I knew the director Robin Hardy and gave him a call. He put me on to Peter Snell, who was about to depart for parts in Scotland. He said the only part left was that of the Librarian, but I could have it if I wanted it. I said I did. A couple of weeks later, my furbelows were under attack by the freezing elements once more.

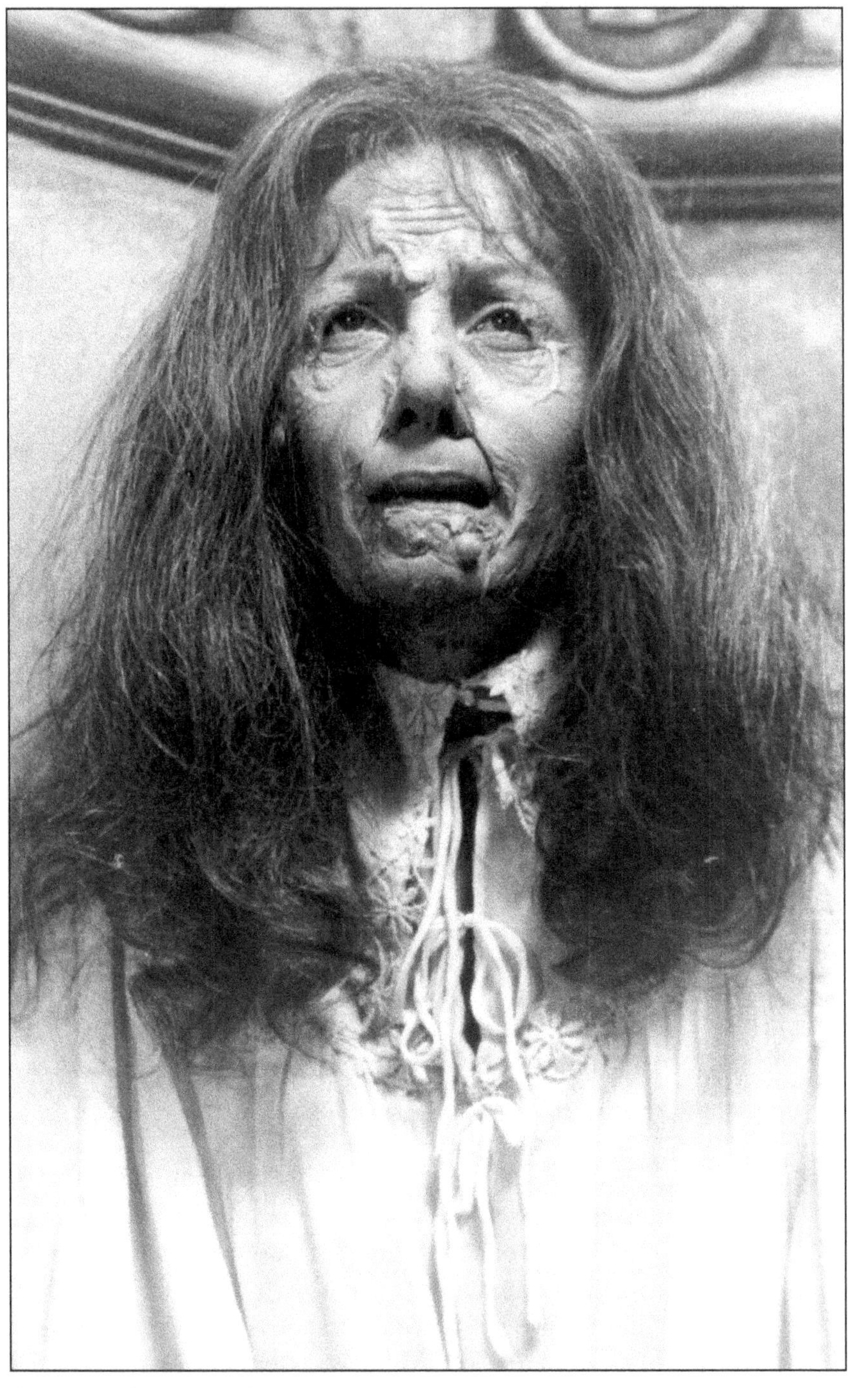

Ingrid in *Countess Dracula*.

Ingrid in *The Wicker Man*.

MATT: Is it true that you worked for next to nothing as far as pay?

INGRID: Christopher did as far as I can remember. I'm afraid my approach to acting is a little more pragmatic. I commit to the job and expect my efforts to be appreciated in the form of cash.

MATT: Why did you want to do this low-budget film?

INGRID: I wanted to do the film because I wasn't working. At that time, that was my main motivation—work!

MATT: The film is like almost nothing I have ever seen, as far as horror films. Did you know right away that this was going to be something unique?

INGRID: I'm sorry. I wish I could say that as soon as I saw the script I was bowled over by the thought of working on it, but I wasn't. I didn't have a lot to do in it except swing my arms and dance a bit. Oh yes! There was the nude bathing scene, of course.

MATT: Of course! How many films have you done where you appeared naked in a bathtub? This film was the second that I have seen. Clearly, you are comfortable with your body and have no problem doing nudity.

INGRID: I have got a bit of a reputation for appearing starkers! But in reality it was only in three films. *Vampire Lovers, Countess Dracula*, and *The Wicker Man*. I was happy with it. Maddie (her *Vampire Lovers* co-star, Madeline Smith) was a bit reserved about it to begin with but soon began flouncing with the best of them. Now there is so much nudity in film, it has lost its impact. It's a shame really.

MATT: Like other films of yours, it had a magnificent location shoot. Where was *The Wicker Man* filmed?

INGRID: It was shot around Dumfries in Scotland. I've been back there to a few festivals since. I even stayed at the same hotel, The Kirroughtree, a lovely place. If you are around that area you should drop in. Mention my name. It could get me a discount next time I go there.

MATT: The film's story takes place in May. I read that production was actually shot in the fall and it was fairly cold and uncomfortable to film at times. Was this true for you?

INGRID: Cold is not the word I would use. The Scots are a hardy breed, and even the hotels at that time had icicles on their icicles, and that was in the bedroom. Apple blossoms had to be brought in to decorate the trees and seduce you into thinking it was a warmer time of the year. I was not that easily seduced. Not by the apple blossoms, anyway.

MATT: Were you present for the actual burning of the Wicker Man statue? And what was it like watching that massive statue go up in flames?

INGRID: Yes! I was there! It did warm the place up a bit. Eddie Woodward came off worse. He was wearing only a nightshirt and his assets were frozen. In between shots, he insisted in sticking his feet under my skirt to warm them up. I thought the way the head of the Wicker Man toppled at the last moment was spectacular.

MATT: Was there anything inside the Wicker Man statue when it was burned? I read that after the film's release many people were upset thinking some animals had actually been crucified?

INGRID: It's a nice gory story, but on a film set, when you do anything with animals, there is always a bunch of RSPCA people standing watching every move. The animals are treated better than the extras.

MATT: Is it true one of the animals urinated on Edward Woodward?

INGRID: It certainly did.

MATT: The film had some trouble getting released. I read that Christopher Lee was very adamant about this film being released. Can you tell me what you know as far as why there were issues releasing the film?

INGRID: Mainly lack of faith, I think. Robin Hardy, Christopher Lee, and Peter Snell were bullish about the film. Unfortunately, the bullishness didn't extend to the moneymen. All through the shoot, there was a game of musical chairs going on in the boardroom of British Lion and there were daily rumors that the film was going to be pulled. Cut to pieces, it was at last reluctantly released as second billing to *Don't Look Now.* Folklore has it that it was on the college campuses of America that the final incantation was said that brought the film to life.

MATT: Do you think if the film had a proper big studio release its initial reception would have been greater?

INGRID: Who knows? A big release doesn't necessarily mean success. Look at the remake with Nicolas Cage.

MATT: What do you think of *The Wicker Man* being hailed as one of Britain's greatest horror movies?

INGRID: I think it is great, especially if they name me, which luckily they do! That bathing scene certainly got noticed.

MATT: Did you see the 2006 remake with Nicolas Cage? What are your thoughts on it?

INGRID: I'm sorry. I didn't see it. But it was hinging to nothing from the start. What I can never understand is why producers want to remake highly successful iconic films in the first place. Or should that be the second place? Why don't they pick out some of the great scripts that have been turned into duff films and remake them better?

A recent portrait of Ingrid.

MATT: Do you have a particular favorite film of yours?

INGRID: I get asked this question a lot and I always feel I'm being a bit pretentious when I say *War and Peace* (the Russian Bondarchuk Edition). The reason you ask? It's the sort of film you can wallow in. It goes on forever. You can drift off, make love, or have a cup of tea and the actors are still there, emoting.

MATT: Lately you have done a lot of writing, with books and columns. Can you tell me how you got involved in writing?

INGRID: I always had this thing about pressing my thoughts on others. Writing is great. You can say your piece and lie back grinning. You don't have to argue your point on the spot. One of my first efforts was a tract about American Indians, or Native Americans, if you prefer. In it I dared to criticize Abraham Lincoln. I thought it was quite reasonable as he was all for getting rid of the people who owned the country. Evidently, that is not how it plays in the USA and foreigners only perform genocide.

MATT: Some actresses don't embrace being a "Scream Queen." In fact, in the UK, I think many consider you the ultimate "Scream Queen." Do you enjoy your title?

INGRID: Well, I'm not too keen on the "Scream" part. I don't think I have ever screamed in a film. I usually provoke the screaming. That's fine with me, but as Mae West said, "I don't care what they say as long as they get my name right."

MATT: Every year in November, you host an annual event in the U.K. Can you tell me about the event? And

can you also tell me about your popular web site
www.pittofhorror.com?

INGRID: My birthday is November 21, if you are thinking
of sending me a card. So, I combine my birthday
with the Fan Club Reunion and throw a dinner
at the Lowiczanka Restaurant in the Polish Centre
in London. I invite a load of my mates from the
film and writing worlds, and we have knees up.
Food's wonderful, company's great, and it is only
15 minutes up the road from where I live. You
can find out all about it on my website at
www.pittofhorror.com. I also mouth my opinions
on it, as well as advertise my dating agency especially
designed for those of a gothic persuasion:
www.ingridpittdateline.com. So is that okay? Can
I sneak off for a quick Bloody Mary now?

MATT: Of course! Thank you Ingrid.

Chapter Ten:
JESSICA HARPER

As an actress, Jessica Harper has appeared in many light-hearted early 1980s films including *Pennies From Heaven, My Favorite Year*, and Woody Allen's *Stardust Memories*. She is well known for her work in the cult films *Phantom of the Paradise* by Brian De Palma and more so Dario Argento's highly praised *Suspiria*. In recent years she has had a successful second career as an author and producer of award winning children's books and CDs.

MATT: Your casting in *Phantom of Paradise* was somewhat the "Hollywood Dream" as far as being cast in a role. Can you share it with me?

JESSICA: Brian (De Palma) found me in an Off-Broadway show. He flew me to Hollywood for a screen test and put me up at the legendary Chateau Marmont. He took me out for dinner with Martin Scorsese, and then gave me the part . . . and I beat out Linda Ronstadt!

MATT: Were you a singer in real life?

JESSICA: I was performing in musicals in New York and singing in nightclubs.

MATT: When the movie came out, it wasn't a box office success. Did it surprise you that it gained a cult following through the years?

JESSICA: What surprised me was that it didn't do better when it opened, not that it developed a loyal following.

MATT: I read that it was as a result of *Phantom of Paradise* that director Dario Argento noticed you as an actress. Is that true?

JESSICA: Yes.

MATT: How did you get the part of Suzy in *Suspiria*?

JESSICA: Dario saw me in *Phantom* and met with me when he came to L.A. for casting. He very kindly entrusted me with the role in *Suspiria.*

MATT: Were you aware before shooting began how violent the content of the movie would be? And did you have any problems with it if you did?

JESSICA: I'm not sure I really computed how much violence there would be, but I figured it was part of the genre, take it or leave it. Sometimes violence has its place . . .

MATT: Were you aware that Dario was inspired in part by the Disney film *Snow White* for color schemes in the movie?

JESSICA: That rings a bell!

MATT: Were the set and the lighting as trippy in person as they appeared on film?

JESSICA: Yes, pretty trippy . . . pretty gorgeous I think. Dario has a great eye.

MATT: What was Dario Argento like as a director? Were you familiar with him as an Italian director?

Jessica with Alida Valli in *Suspiria*.

JESSICA: Dario was a total gentleman, in my experience. He was very respectful of the actors, and very committed to the work.

MATT: Were there any language barriers?

JESSICA: I studied Italian before I went to Italy. And I got up to speed fairly quickly. But still, I will admit that there were moments when I was a little clueless as to what the conversation was.

MATT: Many of the actors in the movie were from different countries and spoke different languages. Did that cause issues?

JESSICA: Not really. We all knew basically what everyone else was saying, even if it was spoken in a foreign language. And the movie was shot without sound, to be dubbed later.

MATT: Since the movie was being dubbed later, you have said in other interviews that they weren't too concerned about noise during filming. Did that create chaos for you? Do you recall any instances?

JESSICA: I remember that someone was building a set while we shot. The hammering was a little distracting! But for the most part, they kept the noise down when the camera was rolling.

MATT: *Suspiria* was Joan Bennett's last theatrical film. What was she like to work with?

JESSICA: Joan was a real "movie star" in the best sense. She was a professional, uncomplaining, punctual, etc. I loved working with her.

MATT: Is it true that Dario Argento played the movie's soundtrack throughout filming? Why did he do that?

JESSICA: He might have? To be honest, I don't quite remember, but it would have made sense, to create a mood on the set.

MATT: Who was the elderly woman playing Helna Markos?

Jessica fights off a bat in _Suspiria_.

JESSICA: I was told she was an ancient prostitute they found on the street!

MATT: What was used for the little white maggots used in one particular scene?

JESSICA: Some of the little white maggots were in fact little white maggots! Luckily, the ones that fell on me were actually grains of rice.

MATT: Is there any particular part of the movie that scares you most?

JESSICA: No. I find that when you act in a movie, it loses its fear factor—you're too close to the material to be frightened by it.

MATT: Was it difficult filming the last scene running in the hall?

JESSICA: That was a little scary, but I only had to do it once!

MATT: At the time of this interview (September 2009) it is being reported that a remake of *Suspiria* is in the works. How does that make you feel?

JESSICA: I think it's interesting. But *Suspiria* is so definitively Dario's movie; I don't know how they can remake it. It will be such a different movie from the original without Dario's presence in the filming process.

MATT: Has anyone contacted you about being involved?

JESSICA: No.

MATT: Does it bother you when Hollywood recycles classic movies?

JESSICA: Not as long as they do it well, giving it a spin that makes it worth revisiting.

MATT: What do you think nowadays when reflecting on your experience with *Suspiria*?

JESSICA: It's an experience I am really grateful to have had; I would not trade it for anything. Making it was a highlight in my life.

MATT: On the lighter side of things, you worked with Woody Allen in two films, *Stardust Memories* and *Love and Death*. What is he like as a director?

JESSICA: I loved my part in *Stardust Memories*. It was one of my favorite things in my career. Woody has a way

A recent headshot of Jessica.
PHOTO COURTESY OF JESSICA HARPER.

of figuring out what an actor has in real life that he/they can use to color the character. He draws that out expertly.

MATT: You also appeared in the comedy classic *My Favorite Year*. That looks like it was a blast to make. Can you share a story or two about your experience filming that movie?

JESSICA: Hey, I got to be in the same room with Peter O'Toole: What could be better?

MATT: Recently you have been focusing on writing. Do you enjoy writing and are you currently working on anything?

JESSICA: I have written many books for children and am now working on a cookbook for adults, which will be out next year from Workman Publishing.

MATT: Where can fans learn more about your writing work?

JESSICA: Fans can go to my website: www.jessicaharper.com

MATT: Thank you for taking the time to do this interview, Jessica. Your time has been greatly appreciated.

JESSICA: You are welcome. Thanks for contacting me.

Chapter Eleven:
MARILYN BURNS

Movie making: isn't it make-believe? So we think. How many times have you heard, "Oh, that's not real; that's just a special effect. The actor is fine." After talking to Marilyn Burns, one might reconsider the thought. There was nothing fake about a lot of Marilyn's performance as Sally in *The Texas Chainsaw Massacre*. A lot of the cuts and bruises, and most importantly the reactions were as real as they come.

With a minimal budget, the director Tobe Hooper couldn't fake it. What you saw was what they, the actors, got: temperatures over 100°, crowded spaces, smelly sets, and smelly wardrobes, too. Gunnar Hansen, who played Leatherface, couldn't wash his costume for the entire run of the shoot for continuity purposes. It was a real-life nightmare at times for the cast. It was that realism that captures audience's attention. Here is my 2009 interview with Marilyn Burns that was done via telephone from her home in Texas.

MATT: When did you start acting?

MARILYN: I had always been into acting. I had taken dance lessons and done all those things you have heard a thousand times before from actresses. In the seventh grade, I was a bookworm and straight-A student. I was in the play, *A Midsummer Night's Dream*. I played Helena and it changed my life. I was so comfortable on stage; I didn't have to be geeky and nervous. I just seemed to be able to get into the part and enjoy it. Soon after, I started

An early headshot of Marilyn.

looking for parts in Texas long before I finished high school. Robert Altman shot *Brewster McCloud* here [in Texas]. One summer off from school, I got a job as a tour guide at the Astrodome. This is where he was shooting the movie. One afternoon, I took my tour group right onto the set. I got to meet all the cast and crew. I almost got fired, but it didn't matter. My whole purpose for being there was to get in the movie. I got a bit part as an extra. I got to meet a lot of great people from Los Angeles and New York.

MATT: How did your involvement with *The Texas Chainsaw Massacre* come about?

MARILYN: I was on the Texas film commission under Preston Smith, in the very beginning. I was very young and had just graduated. The commission was helping bring films to Texas. Sidney Lumet, who did many great films, was directing *Lovin' Molly* with Anthony Perkins, Beau Bridges, and Blythe Danner. I got into that by auditioning for the director. I got a part and it was a real nice part. It was the fourth lead and I was to play, I think, Anthony Perkin's wife. Before filming began, Sidney Lumet called me up and said, "Marilyn, I'm sorry, but in order to get the package of stars I want, this agency wants to have this young unknown named Susan Sarandon. She is going to have to play the part. However, we will let you be a stand-in and you could have a small part. So, I was a stand-in for six-foot tall Blythe Danner and five-foot, seven-inch Susan Sarandon. The crew hated me because I was only five-foot, two-inches. They had to get me an apple box to stand on, which didn't make much difference. A soundman even painted it pink, and that didn't help change the height much! Anyway, while on that movie, Tobe Hooper and Kim Henkel, the director and writer of *The Texas Chainsaw Massacre*, came to the set and were looking around. I was trying to get their attention hollering, 'Hey, young Texan people, I'm a Texan too!" But right in the middle of that, as they were at the craft services table,

Stephen Friedman, who had just done *The Last Picture Show* and was producing *Lovin' Molly*, came up to Tobe and yelled, "Hey do you belong on this set?" And Tobe said, " Uh, well, I uh . . . I was just visiting." Friedman said, "Put that chicken back and get off the set." They actually took his two little chicken wings from him. I was recently at a Q and A with Tobe in Dallas, when they asked me the same question, but I shortened it for them. So, I already infamously knew both Tobe and Kim. We kind of met, if you could call that a meeting. On the film commission, there were some politicians, who were going to throw some money into this non-budget horror movie; I mean little budget, Freudian slip! Excuse me. I don't think they had many hopes for the film. They planned to use it as a tax shelter. I knew about the project, so I auditioned for it. Darn it (Jesting)! I was very delighted to be on board.

MATT: What was the audition like?

MARILYN: I don't remember reading. I remember mostly talking about horror films that I grew up watching. There wasn't much to audition for. It was all action! Maybe I read a few scenes I had with Franklin, but I don't recall. I remember it mostly being an interview with Kim, where we talked a whole lot. And we got to see if we could click.

MATT: Were you familiar at all with Ed Gein, the actual serial killer, who was part of the film's inspiration?

MARILYN: No? Now I know everything! At the time, I really didn't know where they got their ideas. All I knew was it was supposed to be called *Headcheese* or *Scum of the Earth*, and I wasn't sure I wanted to be in either. But I wanted to be in a movie, and starring in one was even better! I just prayed the title would change. The movie was rather strange for its day. And of course later on, I did *Helter Skelter*, which starred Steve Railsback as Charles Manson. About a year or two ago, I was in Cleveland doing an autograph signing. Steven was there signing, too. I said to him, "My God, Steven, after all of these years, we're together again." What really caught my attention was on his table he had different pictures from his career. One of them was a photo of him as Ed Gein. He did that movie, and he played him.

MATT: When you started filming *Texas Chainsaw Massacre*, did you know what you were getting yourself into?

MARILYN: Um? Absolutely not! I think the first week in, we began to know because everything that could go wrong *did*! The heat and all kinds of things happened that were unexpected. We began to see the challenge of this project. It wasn't going to be easy. We started out with the van sequences, which were murder. We didn't have the cutaway van like in some films. We had the whole cast and crew in a stupid van we could barely move in. It was 110°, and we couldn't use the air conditioning because they needed to make sure the sound would be picked up accurately. It was hot, miserable, and tedious, and that was just for the friends driving through Texas! I can't even tell you the amount of tension and time it took to film the hitchhiker's scene, where he's using explosives and cutting Franklin. If we had trouble just doing the bullshit on the road, imagine what it was like when you added another body and tried to do special effects. It was like, "Let's have explosions with gun powder in the van!" Where were our heads? The first night,

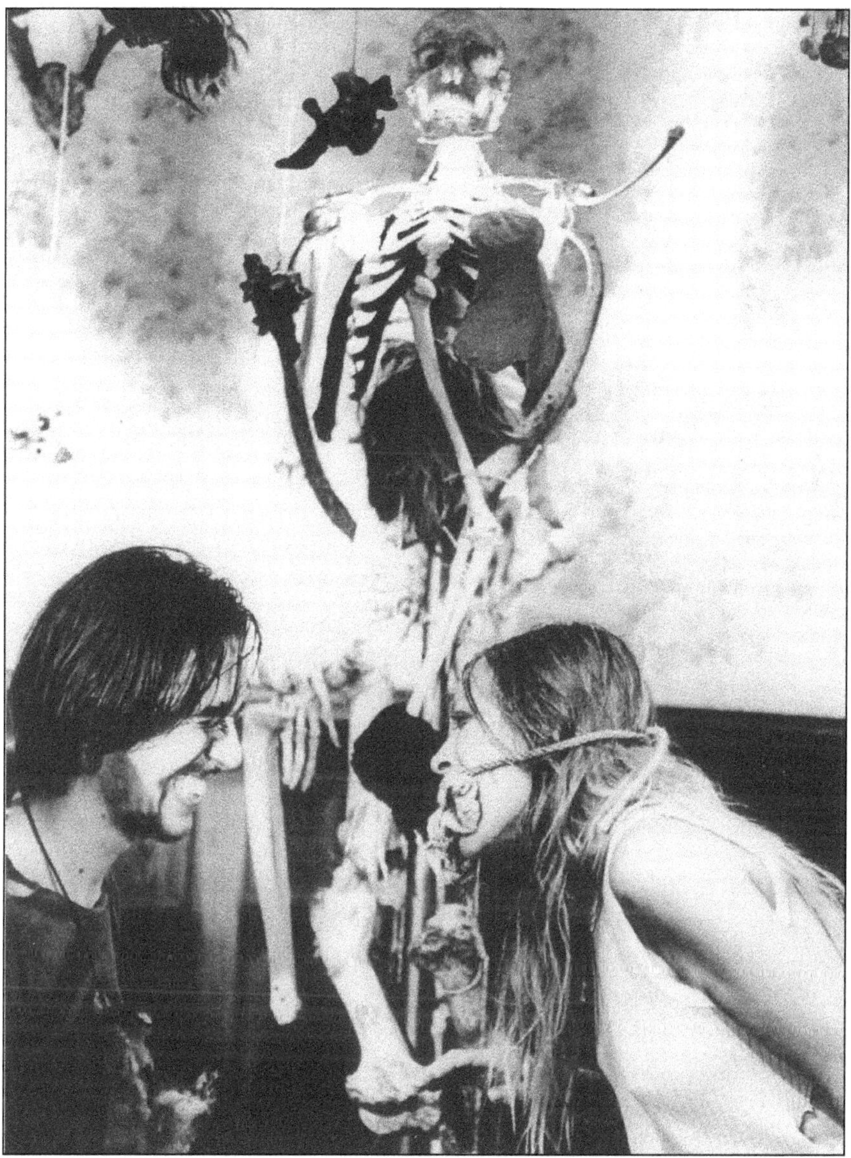

A tied-up Marilyn with co-star Ed Neal in a scene from *The Texas Chainsaw Massacre*.

I was being chased by the chainsaw! I don't think I realized until many years later how dangerously stupid that was. Gunnar tripped once and the chainsaw went up in the air and we all prayed, but, we went right on shooting. It was crazy!

MATT: That's the beauty of low-budget moviemaking.

MARILYN: And it's also when you're kind of young and brainless, which helps a whole lot.

MATT: Well, the van scene in the beginning sets up the mood for the rest of the film, that uncomfortable, hot, eerie feeling. That realism is what makes the movie.

MARILYN: It was real, yes. It was crazy. Oh God! I remember the sausage that Franklin had in his mouth. It was a cooked sausage. We were so unprepared for stupid stuff like that. He kept it in his mouth for days. It was disgusting. That was like the beginning when we thought, "Oh! We're in for some fun times." I knew then that the dinner sequence was going to be a real hoot to shoot!

MATT: Compared with what occurs later in the movie I would think the van sequence would be a walk in the park.

MARILYN: I had forgotten how horrible the van sequence was until recently, when people started asking me questions about it. Teri McMinn, who played Pam, recently said something to me about how she didn't like the way she did the van scene. I told her she was being hard on herself. You know how actors are. She was great. Nothing fazed her. I thought she did a great job in the movie.

MATT: Her character dies in the beginning of the movie, so she didn't have to endure quite as much as you did.

MARILYN: That's a shame because we were always thinking it would have been more fun if she could have hung around longer. She did a damn good job for the time she was in it, and the way she went, that scene took forever. She was probably glad to be done after that scene was shot. She spent a lot of time in a very uncomfortable contraption on a hook. It was very difficult.

MATT: How was that effect done?

MARILYN: Since they didn't have anything to go with Dorothy "Dottie" Pearl, who was the makeup artist, they came up with a way of using pantyhose to hang her. Teri was little enough that she could be held up by a bunch of hose underneath her. What they did was, they wrapped a bunch of pantyhose around her private area, and then they stuck the hose on the hook. Nowadays, I think, in big-budget films, they probably would have done it a different way. You have to realize we were improvising for the moment. They got to that scene and it was like, "Oh man, how are we going to do this?" You come up with all kinds of ways to make it work. It was painful, but it worked. By the way, pantyhose make great rope!

MATT: For a low-budget movie, the art direction was incredible.

MARILYN: Bob Burns did an absolutely exquisite job. The amount of reality that he added to it was awesome. He put his heart and soul into that, just like with everything he did. The man was a genius; I think he started a whole new wave of detail. The movie couldn't have been the movie it was, unless it had all of his touches. My God, what he actually put together and the things he had to go through to get the final results. That poor guy, he had bones from India, poor little kitties, and dogs, which thankfully, we didn't use. In the beginning of the movie, they wanted to have a dead dog on the highway, and then someone protested, "No! Don't ever do that!" Then someone suggested a dead horse. They ended up choosing the armadillo and that—thank God— was what they used. If the film opened with a dead dog or a dead horse, people would have gotten up and left the theater. Heck! I would have. What Robert did was just amazing. The guy was brilliant.

MATT: What was your first reaction when you saw the inside of the family's house?

MARILYN: I was amazed and grossed out. It was disgusting. It was filthy. It was dirty. It was creepy. It gave the perfect effect! I spend more time today checking out pictures and stills and reading about what Robert Burns actually did; I never knew for years how much he put behind it. You know, there's something about being in that environment when you're the victim and you're the actress. You can't fully appreciate it; otherwise, you could creep yourself out. It's only later when you look back at it and realize it's truly an art exhibit.

MATT: Was that house pretty much dilapidated when production started?

MARILYN: No. It really wasn't. It was a nice Victorian house. A family lived there. It's a brilliant old house from the outside. If you watch the film again, you will see how pretty it is. Now, the house is a restaurant in a different town! It must be worth something, because they actually moved it from Round Rock, Texas, to Kingsland, Texas. They held a screening of the film there one summer. I thought no one would show up. I asked my brother, Bill, to take me. I said, "Bill, listen. No one will be there. We'll go, get a good meal, they will screen the movie outdoors, and then we will be on our way home." Or so I thought, right? Well, the place was packed! Driving up the road, leading to the restaurant, I noticed a huge group of people up ahead. I turned to my brother in the car and asked Bill, "What's the big commotion up there?" He said, "Marilyn, I think it's for you." I was amazed. I'm still amazed at how much the movie affects people.

MATT: What was it like the first time you were confronted by Leatherface in the woods with Franklin?

MARILYN: They made sure I didn't see Gunnar until that moment on film. Of course, it scared the crap out of me. I had no clue what to expect. You could read stuff in a script, but it's not the same. I tried to imagine what he would look like. I thought I had some idea, since they were working with makeup on John Dugan. Of course, I didn't. The actual scene was very frightening to do. I'll tell you what was even more frightening than Gunnar: the noise of that chainsaw! I wasn't used to hearing that sound. Those kinds of chainsaws were relatively new. That would get me running. I'll tell you that!

MATT: Was it a real chainsaw?

MARILYN: It was a real chainsaw. All they did was take off the blade. It still had this rubber track that would go round and round while still running. It was really going! You could still get cut. As a matter of fact, to tell you how sharp it was, at the end of the picture when Gunnar is on the ground and the chainsaw hits his leg, he had on a steel plate and several slices of sirloin steak along with his pants and his thermal underwear to protect him. When the chainsaw hit his leg, it cut right through the steak and was going against the steel plate he was wearing. Because of the friction, the steel plate got so hot it burned his leg.

MATT: That night in the woods when you're pushing Franklin in the wheelchair, didn't Tobe antagonize the two of you trying to get you two going at each other's throats?

MARILYN: Oh yes, he told Paul Partain, who played Franklin, a whole bunch of crap that I supposedly said. He told me that Paul said this and that about me, a whole lot of back and forth. Of course, none of it was true. That's not all that helped. Let me start by saying Paul Partain is the sweetest guy in the world. However, all these years, I thought he was Franklin because he never broke character. It wasn't till years ago, when we got together at an autograph signing, he said to me, "You know, Marilyn, I really wanted to be friends with you and all the guys, but I was so afraid if I broke character, y'all might like me, and y'all wouldn't have hate for me, and it would ruin the acting." I thought, *Damn it, Paul.* Do you know what he would do? On set, Tobe would yell "cut," and Paul would look over at me and say, "Sally, get me a Coke. Sally quickly, get me a Coke!" I would say back to him, "Paul, get off your ass. You're not really crippled, get your own Coke." And all he would continue saying is, "Please Sally, Sally get me a coke." It would drive me crazy.

MATT: So he was a method actor.

MARILYN: No one knew that then. We all hated him for twenty years! However, he was a sweetheart of a guy, and yet Tobe did those little tricks to pit us against each other. If you watch the movie, just think about being with someone like that for twenty-four hours straight.

MATT: Sally and Franklin had an interesting relationship. On one hand you can tell she couldn't stand him, yet she was the one always wheeling him around and caring for him.

MARILYN: What can you do? You know, I mean pushing him during those scenes in the woods was damn near impossible. It took every bit of strength and then some, to push him over the roots and branches. I thought, "My God! He gained 300 pounds! I can't do this." Again, that's something you can't foresee by just reading in a script.

MATT: I was surprised when I watched the DVD with your commentary, a few times you actually shrieked in horror. Since you made the film and were there, I didn't think you would still be surprised by anything.

MARILYN: The thing that still scares me no matter how many times I watch the darn movie is when I'm pushing Franklin through the woods and there is that silence and all of a sudden comes that loud chainsaw noise and the horrible scene that follows. That in my mind is so scary. Just use your mind to think about how horrible that is. That being said if I hadn't been in the scene, I probably would have been dying laughing watching Tobe Hooper and Dottie Pearl spit blood onto Leatherface's apron. That's how they did that effect.

MATT: Can you elaborate?

MARILYN: Tobe and Dottie were on their knees just off camera. Once the chainsaw made contact with

Franklin, they started spitting out this fake blood. It's gross to think about, but also kind of funny. I didn't really laugh at the time because I was trying to stay in character. Nowadays, when the cast comes together and I hear Tobe recollect this story with glee, I think to myself, *There must have been some good times had on that film? I just don't remember them.*

MATT: A lot of the time, Tobe changed the script, almost daily. Was it difficult to keep on top of things?

MARILYN: Yes. I have the original script, and there were always pages written in. I was looking at it the other day. There were a lot of changes—some subtle, some big—but there was always a reason why it was changed. You got to remember every shot. Even today's soap opera people, they memorize their stuff at night, go to work the next morning, and there are twenty-two pages of rewrites. The thing with low budget horror movies is that you got to have everybody ready and on their feet. That adds to the intensity and craziness of the film.

MATT: Considering everything you were already going through?

MARILYN: Absolutely. It ended up working; which was good. When you take chances, you keep second guessing those changes, but you always make it work. One makes suggestions of course, a lot of times with me, I didn't have a say. For instance, when I was in the chair and Ed was leering at me. I'm tied to the chair with my hands and I have that disgusting gag that they had just found on set somewhere and crammed in my mouth. I'm making like I'm trying to get away from him and the chair falls over and hits the floor and I heard, "Damn, she went out of the shot!" I'm lying there on the floor and they're ignoring me. I hear, "Well we got enough. Let's go to the next shot. Get the girl!" I'm there, bound and gagged on the floor, and they say, "Get the girl." I knew not to express myself too much. I kind of felt like, *Well, maybe this is helping my character?* It wasn't a very friendly environment.

MATT: Do you think Tobe did a lot of that intentionally?

MARILYN: No. I think it's called, "We're in a hurry and we have to get this shot!" He's not going to stop after I fall out of his shot and say, "Oh little Marilyn, are you hurt?" I don't think so. In fact, when I tell these stories at events and Tobe is on stage with me, you can just see him light up. He laughs and chuckles. He gets a big kick out of it all.

MATT: Let's talk about the infamous dinner scene. Is it true they kept filming for hours on end because Jim Siedow had to leave production?

MARILYN: No. We were losing our light. Come to think of it, I don't remember? We might have had to round it up because Jim had to leave for another shoot. I remember us just trying to get it done. Is that what they say?

MATT: Yes. Jim's contract was about to end?

MARILYN: Oh yes. I'm sure he had already gone days over. He had already been worked overtime and everything enough. We had to get it. And, of course, Tobe wanted to shoot it from every angle you could imagine. I think they shot it from the front of the table, my angle, Jim's angel, Ed's angle, and a few different angles of Leatherface. And that does take a while. I just know the final result from the editing really worked. The worst part of it was the smell. My goodness the smells and odors in that room were the worst. From the rotting chicken that was the centerpiece, to the headpiece, and to the other meats sitting there for days. Gunnar's costume also really smelled. He only had one outfit that he wasn't able to clean obviously. Everybody in that room was hot and sweaty. It was unbearable at times. Many people ran outside cause they were getting ill.

MATT: It isn't often on movies that the set pieces start to decompose.

MARILYN: Yes, that makes it really tough. And you're sitting there thinking, 'What's that smell?' You can't do anything about it. You can't just throw out the set pieces that have already been filmed. You would ruin the continuity. There's just nothing you could do. You're not going to get some Febreeze and spray it in there.

MATT: Was it really hard filming the dinner scene?

MARILYN: Yes. It was just one long shoot. It's exactly how it looks.

MATT: If this movie had a big budget, I don't think the movie would have worked as well.

MARILYN: No. It wouldn't have. We would have been too comfy and enjoying ourselves.

MATT: Were you and Jim Siedow friends?

MARILYN: That's one of the finest men and actors I have ever met in my life. We didn't know each other before the film started, but we certainly remained friends for a very long time after. I was very good friends with his wife Ruth after Jim left us. They were the most charming, wonderful, terrific people you could ever meet. Jim put up with all of us. And you know, God, what a trooper he was. Out of everybody there, he had really been there, done it, been doing it, and was brilliant at it. You have got to say a big thank you to Jim for hanging in there with a bunch of kids and giving it his all. It paid off for him though. Bless him. He got to be in the sequel. And he really got some money for it! I'm so glad that Jim and I got to do some autograph signings together. That meant a lot to me. He would always whisper to me, "I'll be darned Marilyn, who would have thought? Not us!" Then he would laugh. He was a special person.

MATT: In one scene, Jim is hitting you repeatedly with a broom. Didn't he have a hard time shooting that scene?

MARILYN: Yes. He had a lot of trouble in the gas station where he was supposed to be beating me with the broomstick. They had taken the handle off of the broomstick and replaced it with plastic, which actually hurt more than that wood. It really hurt and Jim, the nice guy he was kept pulling his punches, so to speak. After a few takes, Tobe got frustrated about it and yelled "Hit the damn woman!" Jim said, "I can't hit her; I'm sorry, I just can't hit her." Soon, we started losing the light, and people were getting nasty. It was looking like it was going to be another all-nighter. Finally, I said (raises her voice), "Jim, just go ahead and hit me already, or we will never get out of here. We will be here forever. Let's get it over with!" He said, "Marilyn you sure?" and I said, 'Jim do it!' I was so tired I didn't care at that point. I wanted to go

Marilyn in a scene from *The Texas Chainsaw Massacre*.

home. And when he hit me, it knocked me down and gave me a black eye. But we got the shot and it looked good and I can tell you he didn't pull it. That was real.

MATT: It looked painful!

MARILYN: It was! We were spending the whole night trying to do this one scene and after a while your whole body, from screaming and fighting. It gets unbearable! I just wanted to go home. We could see the light coming in through the little cracks of the panel. Heck, I think the gas station had to be open for business at a certain time too! We had to get out of there.

MATT: Aside from that scene, you really took a beating throughout production. Can you tell me some more instances?

MARILYN: I'll tell you one of the things that I did not realize until just a few years ago. I was doing a question and answer with Gunnar and the cast. I was in the middle of telling a story about how the prop knife one time didn't work. They accidentally cut me in one scene and I actually bled. Halfway through the story, I don't know what came over him, but Gunnar, after all these years interrupts and says to me, "Marilyn, come on, don't tell that story anymore. It wasn't that the prop knife didn't work. It didn't mess up. We just decided to cut you." I looked at him and thought, *All these years, I have been saying he accidentally cut me, but, no! They really cut me and knew they were going to before they shot it!* When he said that, I just about died. I thought, *You have got to be kidding me.* I felt betrayed for a very short minute.

MATT: So for all those years, you thought it was an accident?

MARILYN: Yup, all those years. I always said it was an accident until maybe about five years ago. I remember him interrupting me saying that, and again you can see Tobe light up and laugh. And then there was my hair. Just trying to get all that syrup and stuff out of my hair for days was impossible. After a few days, I was making progress with my hair. I'm thinking that life is going forward. I thought I was done with filming this movie. I needed to be done. My phone rang and it was Tobe. "Marilyn, we lost the footage. It didn't work. We have to shoot the ending again." Are they serious? I thought I had worn that disgusting outfit for the last time. That is why I am so absolutely real in the end. I was going crazy!

MATT: That hysterical laugh was real, wasn't it?

MARILYN: I think so. I mean, come on. It was beyond therapy! It was the fact that I thought I had finished it. I was done! They can't screw it up again. We have got to be finished. But then you never knew. Then they'd call. It drove you into mad laughter.

MATT: You also had a limp in the last scene. Was that real?

MARILYN: In one scene towards the end, Sally jumps out of the window in an attempt to escape. They had brought in a stunt girl to shoot part of the scene, and me to shoot the other. The stunt girl was brought in to jump through the glass. She got off easy. What she was to do was jump through a sugar glass window. Lucky for her, it was all level. She didn't have to jump down any stories. She was making a leap from one side of the window to the other. That was all, no fall. What they did with me, they brought in this scaffolding. It must have been about six or eight feet high. No less than six feet. It was shot very early in the morning. I remember when they yelled, "action" and I jumped down. They started throwing the sugar glass at me from behind to give the effect that I had just jumped out of the window. The thing was because of the humidity in Austin the sugar glass started to really harden. It felt like crystals were being pelted at the back of my head. It hurt. When I landed on the ground, there is a shot of me and you can see it in my face. In my brain, I was thinking, *Did I just break my ankle?* Luckily, I didn't. I just sprained it. We had to shoot the end of the movie differently because of my limp. Originally, I was going to be running away from them at full speed. But because of my foot Tobe had Gunnar and Edwin sort of dancing and twirling around. Otherwise, the movie would have been over in a heartbeat.

MATT: When you finally finished the movie, was it a hard transition back to everyday life?

MARILYN: No. It was just hard to get my hair back in good condition. It was never over for a while because Tobe would call me and say, "Marilyn, I just need a few minutes of your time. I just need a shot of your eye." I said, " few minutes? Okay fine." I would get there and, of course, three or four hours later, I'm still there. They are shooting an extreme close up of my eyeball. After a few hours, without cleaning them, puss starts coming out. It was gross. However, it was good for the film. But, I didn't know my eye was going to be the entire screen in the end.

MATT: Was there anything hardest for you to shoot?

MARILYN: They were all equally challenging. Whether it was running in the woods and having branches and thorns hit me, or trying to jump in the back of the pickup truck at the end. God, it felt like it took twenty-seven takes to do that jump. Try jumping into the back of a pickup truck when you're only five-foot, two, and in the middle of the Texas sun. It's not easy. I can't say that about any shot. "Oh, that was a piece of cake, or that was so difficult." I think they were all equal opportunities of pure hell.

MATT: What did you think was going to happen with the film once it was finished? It was like nothing ever shown on the big screen before!

MARILYN: I just wanted it to get on the screen and my scenes not get left on the cutting room floor. Those were the two things I cared about: *please go to the movies* and *please don't cut me*. Once I realized I wasn't cut, I was happy. Still, the first time I saw it, I just kept thinking to myself, *Don't cut me. God, please don't cut me.* I think it's because so many other movies I had been in my scenes were cut. I was so happy when it got into theaters. Before I knew it, it was on Hollywood Boulevard, I just thought it was amazing.

MATT: What did your friends and family think of the movie when they saw it?

MARILYN: Well, my Mom and Dad took the bridge club and some of their friends to see it. Afterwards, Mom and Dad called and said, "Marilyn, nobody said anything. They just sat there." I said to my parents, "Nobody said anything?" They replied, "Nope Marilyn, nobody." I said, "I guess that's good. Maybe they were so stunned." I think the bridge club went to the movies one or two more times with my parents. But pretty soon, they all stopped going to the movies together.

MATT: *The Texas Chainsaw Massacre* is one of the most successful film franchises out there. Have you seen any of the other films?

MARILYN: Yes, I have. I remember going to the one that had Jessica Biel in it. They said it was going to be an exact replica of the original. I went by myself, because I couldn't get anyone to go with me. I was nervous for whatever reason. I thought, after a while, this isn't like my movie. This is okay. They did a good job, but it wasn't exactly the same as they said it was going to be.

MATT: You also had a cameo in one of the films.

MARILYN: Kim, who wrote the original, was the writer for *The Return of the Texas Chainsaw Massacre*. It starred Renee Zellweger and Matthew McConaughey. They gave me a part and I wanted it real bad. I was going to be a nurse. I was real excited about it. The problem was that the movie wasn't a SAG project. I'm a member of the Screen Actors Guild. They said I could do it, but they would have to dub my voice. I thought that I wasn't going to do something and then have my voice dubbed. I told Kim, "Look, I'll play some stupid little part. It'll be an inside joke between us. I'll be lying down on a gurney, and no one will know." I didn't wear makeup or anything. I messed up my hair and all I did was just passed through real quickly on the gurney. I thought no one would ever know. Then, I was doing these autographs shows and people would come up to me saying, "Hey you were in *Texas Chainsaw 5*!" I thought it was going to be a background funny joke amongst friends. Who knew it wouldn't be anonymous?

MATT: Why did SAG want to dub your voice?

MARILYN: It wasn't a SAG project. I'm a union actor. They don't like you doing that sort of thing. That's why no one liked *Chainsaw* when it first came out. It was considered a SCAG film, since it was done independently. SAG still doesn't like non-union films. Of course nowadays, with Internet taking over, all your best young filmmakers are coming out regardless.

MATT: Some of the cast felt like they got short ended on money. Do you share any of that feeling?

MARILYN: Well, in the beginning, it looked like it was making this great fortune. We later found out that Bryantson Pictures was connected to the mafia and they basically stole it from us. They weren't going to give us any money. I have the papers of how much the movie grossed. According to the mafia, "It didn't do nuttin." But it did plenty. Let's put it this way, we might not have gotten paid back then, but we have certainly been paid and recognized now. That makes it worthwhile. It would have been nice to get our slice of the pie. But going up against the mafia there isn't much you can do. Thankfully, they got the distribution rights to the movie back.

MATT: Has *Texas Chainsaw Massacre* caused you to miss out on work?

MARILYN: Yes, of course it has. It wasn't recognized for many years as a classic. There was one article in the *Los Angeles Times* that was almost a whole page. It read in big letters, "SLEAZE" with a big picture of me screaming right next to the big letters. So, if you see that and then I come into your office for a job and you never saw the movie, you don't know what to think. I was judged because of that. I went to see this director one time, and this one really got me. It's somebody we know. He said, "Marilyn, I don't blame you for doing it. You're an actress and that's how you make a living. But . . . ." He then said, "I took my thirteen-year-old to see *The Texas Chainsaw Massacre.*" I'm thinking, *What the hell are you thinking? Didn't you read a review?* I didn't say anything to him, but here he was giving me this nasty lecture about it. I did say, "Look, can I audition now for the movie? That's why I'm here." He said, "No. I just wanted to meet you." It's good and bad. Just good and bad.

MATT:

Do you remember what the general response to the movie was?

MARILYN:

When it came out, people booed at the screen, people got sick, people went crazy over it. Rex Reed said—and Rex Reed was really big at the time—"Run, don't walk. It makes *Psycho* look like a nursery rhyme and *The Exorcist* look like a comedy." That was excellent. Johnny Carson was on TV saying it was the most despicable, horrible, vile thing you could ever see. Women Against Violence asked me, "Why, Ms. Burns, would you do such a movie?" I told them, "I got away. I'm the only victim to ever get away! I'm a heroine. Don't you get it?" And then, there was this little tidbit . . . "Psychologically, the way perverts see these movies is to get out their aggression." That came from some *San Francisco Chronicle.* Another review read, "*Chainsaw* is the epitome of people that are sick and mentally ill and they need some avenue to release it, otherwise they would be serial killers." So, there was definitely a mixed reaction to the film.

MATT:

What do you think about meeting the fans at autograph shows?

MARILYN:

Absolutely wonderful! Can you think of a better way to spend the weekend? What could be more fun? I go to New York City, Los Angeles, all of these wonderful cities and meeting the greatest fans. I'm very blessed. It's always nice seeing Gunnar, Ed, and all of them at conventions. It's a blast!

MATT:

For many years, Teri McMinn, who played Pam, distanced herself from the movie. Recently, she has come out of her self-imposed exile.

MARILYN: She certainly has and she is a ball to be around.

MATT: Do you think she is enjoying all the attention she is getting now?

MARILYN: Who wouldn't? She just didn't know how much fun it would be. She didn't know what to expect.

MATT: After *Texas Chainsaw Massacre*, you did *Helter Skelter.* How did that come about?

MARILYN: By then, I had moved to California and got an agent. I brought my pictures to everybody in town, and I handed them out one by one. I auditioned for the role. At the time, people didn't want to see the movie made. Hollywood was still thinking it was too soon. Actors and actresses were passing up on it left and right, but my agent decided he would send me. I had to go because of my agent. If I didn't go I would have felt like I was being disrespectful to him. Plus, who was I not to go? I had my reservations about it. I knew you had to shave your head to be in it. All of Manson's girls had to shave their heads. I went in for the audition and I said, "I'm here to audition, but I really don't want to shave my head." Tom Gries, the director said, "Good. Then you could read for Kasabian." That was the best part. So I read for him. I thought I did terribly. So, I went home that night and I cried. I was lying there in bed crying, thinking I should go home to Texas. Just then, my agent called, just like in the movies. He said, "Marilyn, you got the part." Then, of course, I cried harder.

MATT: For a television movie to have such a following after all of these years, really says something about it. Most television movies simply come and go. Not too many have staying power.

Marilyn as Linda Kasabian in *Helter Skelter*.

MARILYN: That is another blessed event. I knew it was hot then. It was the #1 miniseries at the time. Then *Roots* came along, and I thought, *Oh well*. But it's still fresh in people's minds. It's another one of those things.

MATT: Was it different for you, as an actress, to play a role based on a real life person versus a character?

MARILYN: Well, yes. Especially since Linda was there both nights of the murders, and yet she's being Rebecca of Sunnybrook Farm, as she is testifying. It was very hard. But you know they needed a little angel. Even the writer of *Helter Skelter*, Vincent Bugliosi, knew they needed an angel to get the others convicted. You've got to have one credible witness. And they superimpose the murders on my face. She was what they needed to get the rest of them in jail.

MATT: Did you do any research on her or the Manson murders when you got the part?

MARILYN: I did a ton of research, on everybody. But I certainly didn't want to meet any of them. That wasn't my idea of a good time had by all.

MATT: Did Linda Kasabian ever try and contact you?

MARILYN: Heck no. My only brush with anything like that was on set. We were shooting at the Paramount ranch and some extra came up to me unannounced and dug her nails into my arm. She looked at me and said, "Linda wasn't there that day." Obviously, it was one of Charlie's friends. That scared me. Another day, I remember looking up at the mountainside where we filmed and seeing guys dressed up with guns. They looked like SWAT members. I said, "Hey Tom (our director) . . . why is there a SWAT team up over there? Those people have guns?" Tom said, "Marilyn, there was a bomb threat." There were some people that weren't happy we were making the movie.

MATT: Steve Railsback as Charles Manson was absolutely terrifying. You couldn't take your eyes off him.

MARILYN: He was just brilliant.

MATT: It was chilling to watch on TV. What was it like being in the courtroom and having him stare you down?

MARILYN: He was chillingly effective. He was amazing to watch, as you see from his performance. If you were lucky enough to be in the room it was just surreal. You didn't need to worry about staying in character. He was so real. He took you with him.

MATT: Does it surprise you that the film has had a lasting effect on people?

MARILYN: No. There are some reasons why. Steve's performance alone makes it stand out as a movie. Also, the subject matter was a chilling, *real life* documentary and one of the first of its kind. I can certainly find it a lot more credible than good old *Chainsaw*, which is amazing.

MATT: You worked with Tobe Hooper again on *Eaten Alive.* What was that like?

MARILYN: An experience. It was very different from the first time around. We were on a big soundstage at the studio. It was big enough that cars were able to drive on and off set. I remember the pond, where the little gator was, once flooded the entire set. We couldn't work for a while because then the prop alligator got full of water and sank to the bottom and we had to dry him out. There were the same old little problems you would get. But the budget was definitely better. The spider monkey shared a dressing room next to mine. I didn't find that very funny, but the crew did, of course. My dressing room was just four walls, a cubicle, and it had no roof. I would be in there changing and all the camera men and crew would be up on top adjusting lights or whatnot and I would just wave to them. It was a fun experience.

MATT: Who was in that one with you?

MARILYN: The actors were marvelous: Carolyn Jones, Neville Brand, Stuart Whitman, Bill Finley, and little Kyle Richards. There were just so many good people to work with and learn from.

MATT: The movie had it seems like hundreds of titles before they finally decided upon *Eaten Alive.* Do you remember any of the previous titles?

MARILYN: I'm amazed at how many titles it has had. It was many things from *Starlight Slaughter* to *Death Trap* to *Brutes and Savages* to *Legend of the Bayou* to *Horror Hotel*, to finally, *Eaten Alive!* The movie is alive and well to this day. People are still asking me to sign stuff from it. People really like it.

MATT: When you started out as an actress, did you foresee yourself becoming an actress most associated with horror movies?

MARILYN: No (laughs). I always considered myself a Shakespearean actress. I knew all the classics. I studied the treasures of the theater. Never in my wildest dreams did I think I would be known for horror. But I am proud of it. It just wasn't the plan.

MATT: Anything you wanted—excuse me—want to do?

MARILYN: Many different things. I know I missed out on certain roles because of the association with horror. I also turned down a few projects, because it was the same kind of stuff. For a while it seemed like the same thing, over and over again was being offered to me. I kind of wish now, I had gone ahead and done some of them. But, back then there weren't that many horror films, or "Scream Queens." It wasn't what it is today. In fact, when they came up with that title "Scream Queen" I thought, *No, please don't call me that.* Now, of course, I realize it's not the way I perceived it.

MATT: Does the "Scream Queen" label still bother you?

MARILYN: No. I think it's kind of amusing and funny. Look, if someone had to start it I'd rather it be me and Jamie Lee Curtis, because that's who they say were

Marilyn, as Linda Kasabian, and cast members of the TV-movie _Helter Skelter_, starring Steve Railsback as Charles Manson.
PHOTO COURTESY OF JOHN "DOC" STRANGE.

the first "Scream Queens," is Jamie and I. And heck, I do give them a run for their money in that particular area of expertise.

MATT: Do you personally enjoy the macabre?

MARILYN: Yes. Well, I have always liked mysteries, detective, horror movies and books. But not if I'm alone by myself. If I'm alone and _Nightmare on Elm Street_ comes on TV, I have to turn it off. At one o'clock in the morning, I'm not going to start turning on all my lights and checking the bathroom and the damn closets to see if Freddy is in there. I can't do it; I have to turn it off. I had to go watch _The Exorcist_ seven times in order to see the whole movie. Every time Mercedes McCambridge started talking, I would cover my eyes with a scarf. That voice of hers scared me to death.

MATT: Looking back do you have a favorite role?

MARILYN: I have a lot of favorites, different plays, there are parts I have always loved and I still know the lines today. Don't get me started there's so many characters that are just wonderful from Tennessee Williams to Eugene O'Neill. Just so many different characters come to my head and I thoroughly enjoy them. Each film was an experience unto itself. An experience I really enjoyed and appreciated.

MATT: I read online you do a lot of theater these days.

MARILYN: I keep up with everything. This year, I have been doing so many conventions I have been away from home, more than I have been home and that's been a lot of fun.

MATT: It's also been a lot of fun talking with you, Marilyn. Thank you for talking with me.

MARILYN: You're welcome, Matthew.

Chapter Twelve:
BETSY PALMER

How does one go from being best known as a game show panelist, to being best known as cinema's most murderous momma? You need a new car. At least that was the case with Betsy Palmer. If you told Betsy Palmer thirty years ago that she would be best remembered for what she referred to as "a piece of shit film," she would have told you that you were crazy. The release passed its thirtieth anniversary and Betsy Palmer is no doubt best known for her appearance as the knife-wielding Mrs. Voorhees, a fate she has slowly come to accept in her later years.

With a new installment of the *Friday the 13th* series coming out what seems like every six months, Betsy Palmer is sure to keep garnering new generations of devotees. I had the honor of speaking to Betsy Palmer on Mother's Day, May 19, 2009. This was one Mother's Day I will not soon forget.

MATT: First of all, I would like to thank you for talking to me on Mother's Day. What a thrill to talk to cinema's most murderous momma.

BETSY: Well, listen, I think every day is Mother's Day.

MATT: I want to get right into it since we have limited time on this Mother's Day together. Is it true you only accepted the role in *Friday the 13th* because you needed a new car?

BETSY: I did! Yes. I was working on Broadway. I can't remember which show that I was in at the time. I was driving home after the show. I was living in Connecticut, and my car just crapped out on me. It just stopped! And I wasn't even sure whether I was still in New York or Connecticut. Anyway, what happened was there I am, the car has just stopped, and I'm stuck. A man pulls up behind me in a car. He asked, "What's the problem?" I said, "I don't know. I can't start the car; it just stopped." And mind you, this was in the days before cell phones. So the gentleman said, "Let me take you to a telephone." So, he took me to one. I made a call to AAA and they said, "Where are you?" I told them that I wasn't sure. I'm on I-95 somewhere. They said, "Okay, we'll send a car out." So, I walked back maybe a quarter of a mile, and here I am walking with my theater make-up on. I probably looked like some "ho" along I-95, a major highway. Trucks were honking the horn as I'm walking back to my car. You know, when you want the police to show up, you hope they will, but they never do.

MATT: Right.

BETSY: Finally, a young guy arrived in his truck. My car was a Mercedes. It was one that I had for many years. And the thing about a Mercedes is that it cannot be pulled from the front, only from the back. At least that's the way my car was. So, we pushed the car off to the side of the road. There wasn't anything that he could do. He was about to drive off on me, when I said, "Well, could you please give me a lift, at least to Greenwich so I can catch the train home?" He obliged. The poor guy probably had a date. He couldn't wait to get out of there! I got home and I said to my daughter, "I have got to get a new car. I can't just depend on this one anymore." She said, "Why don't you get a Volkswagen? They have a car called a Scirocco. It's cute, it's small, and it's sporty." I went to see the car and I liked it a lot. It was priced $9,999. It was just under $10,000. Now, we are talking many years ago. We're not talking about the prices of cars today. Later that week, my agent called and said, "How would you like to do a movie?" I said "Great! I haven't done a movie in years. Does it shoot in California?" He said, "No. It's going to be shot over in Jersey. It's ten days' work, and they will pay you $1,000 a day." I said, "Whoopee!! That means I could buy the car." He said, "There's one drawback." I said "What's that?" He said, "It's a horror movie." I said, "Oh, no. Oh, God. It's bad enough I'm known as a game show player on television, and now a horror film! No I can't do that, sorry." Then, I thought about the car again. I told my agent to send me the script. He sends me this script, I read it, and I said. "What a piece of shit. Nobody will ever see this movie! It will come and it will go. It's just going to be what, ten days of work for me? It's only twenty minutes of screen time." I called my agent back and said, "Fine, I'll do it." As I was driving to the set, there was this sign that read, Crystal Lake. It was where I was to turn off into the woods and get to the Boy Scout camp. I thought to myself, *Oh, that might be a good omen*. I had spent my childhood from the age of two until I was about ten at a lake in Warsaw, Indiana, called Crystal Lake. Who knew? I did my ten days work and bought my car.

Matt: And you had a dollar left over.

Betsy: (Laughs). Yes!

MATT: Wasn't there some backlash for you after doing the role of Mrs. Voorhees? I read that one critic published your address.

BETSY: Oh yes! Those two guys! One of them died. They were over in Chicago. It was one of them who said, "How dare Betsy Palmer do a movie like that, with the image she has given us all these years." I never met the guy. But I heard that through the grapevine. He thought that I should not have done the movie. He was very upset that I did it. I figure that I'm an actress, and an actress can do all kinds of roles.

MATT: Do you get upset at negative remarks made by critics?

BETSY: Well, as they say, "Those who can do, do. Those who can't, criticize."

MATT: Did you embrace the movie once you were on set?

BETSY: It really was just a role. I dismissed it once I finished it. I did what I did with her and it was fun. There was nobody else on the film by the time I got there. It was the end of film. It was just Adrienne King and I.

MATT: Well, that's because you killed everyone.

BETSY: (Laughs). Yes. I saw the movie once and then didn't see it for many years. There was a showing here in New York City, and all the people who had been in it came to a little screening of it. I looked at it and I was right. I knew it was crap. I never looked at it again.

MATT: Do you still think it's a piece of crap?

Betsy on the attack in *Friday the 13th*.

BETSY: No. I finally, finally . . . I think the last time I saw it was at a convention. They were going to be screening the film. After the screening, they had me up on stage doing questions and answers with the audience. When they came to get me from the table where I was signing autographs, they took me to the screening room. I had to watch the last few minutes of the film. I thought to myself, "Hmm, that's not such a bad acting job at all. I think I did a pretty god job." And I made peace with it. At that point, I had to, especially the way people love it. I do autograph signings all the time, especially horror conventions, and the people just love Mrs. Voorhees. They carry babies in their arms. They have me hold their babies. When we take pictures, the fans want me to put my hands around their necks like I'm strangling them. It becomes a big romp. It really does. I enjoy it. I'm easy with meeting strange people. I should say strangers (laughs)!

MATT: With all you had accomplished up until that time and forward, does it get you that *that's* what you will perhaps be known for forever?

BETSY: I have accepted it with peace in my heart. To tell you the truth, I am honored that the people feel that way about me. It isn't only because I'm an actress doing an acting job. I think something in the performance came through. I think the audience understood why I killed those people. I tried to keep the camp closed. I approached it like I would approach every role I approach. I learned the Stanislavski method. A Russian director taught me.

MATT: So you developed Mrs. Voorhees?

BETSY: When I was looking at the script, there was one shot of a hand that had a man's high school ring on it. Back in the day, we all went steady in high school. This was in the 1940s and you always wore your boyfriend's ring, usually with a bunch of tape wrapped around it because it's too big, or one would put it on a chain and wear it like a necklace around your neck. I thought, *Okay.* This is when I decided I would do the role and started to think about who she was as a person and what her background must have been to make her do these terrible things. I made up this story. The story was as follows: back then, we didn't go to bed. In those days, girls were nice girls, but there was always one girl in school that would go all the way. In my school, it was Betty June Stubbs. I even remember her name. At least Betty June said she did. Who knows if she did or not? Okay, here I am. I am going steady with this guy in high school. We get carried away at one point in time and make love. I became pregnant and told him about it. He said, "Oh, don't put it on me!" And that was the end of the relationship. I didn't say anything about it at home for as long as I could. And of course, I started showing the pregnancy. Finally, I have to admit to my father that I'm pregnant. My father immediately throws me out of the house and said, "Get out! You're no daughter of mine, you slut!" He said terrible things to her. Here I am a young girl not even graduated from high school and I have no way of earning a living. So, I started doing all these little odd jobs to get by on. Mrs. Voorhees was even going to the Salvation Army and getting what she could. It was not easy for her. She finds a home for unwed mothers and that's where I figured she had the child. So now, here she is with this little kid and she is really struggling. She wants to be the best mother she can be for little Jason. Finally, there is a ray of sunshine. There is an ad for a job to be a cook at a camp for young children. I thought (as Mrs. Voorhees) *How wonderful, my little boy will be able to be with other children and I'll be there making money and we will have a nice place for the summer.* She goes to work at the camp and what happens there? Well, the young counselors who are in love go off and make love somewhere leaving the children unattended. And my boy ultimately drowns in the lake. That is when, after everything this gal had gone through, she just snapped and does all that stuff. That was my justification for her and that's how I played her.

MATT: They should make that into a prequel for *Friday the 13th*. That's a great story.

BETSY: Well, that's how I work on every role. My teacher always said, "You always had a life before you walked on stage or in front of a camera." So, I made up her life. Perhaps that's what comes through. They wanted me to do more of them, but I didn't want to. I did some voiceovers for the second one. Because the guy that directed it, Steve Miner, had been our assistant director or something on the first one. So. I did it as a favor. But time and time again, they wanted me to come back. I wouldn't do it. I never got any residuals, you know, not a dime.

Matt: Even for a film in the 1980s?

Betsy: I think it was soon after they went into the residual thing. Would have made a few bucks there. But I made enough to buy the car.

Matt: Do you still have the car or know what became of it?

Betsy: No (laughing). I gave it to my daughter, eventually.

Matt: In all the new movies, who is this Jason killing all these people? Isn't he dead?

Betsy: I say that all the time, especially when I am at the autograph shows. I always tell them, "That's not my son. My son is dead. I never would have done those things if my little boy hadn't drowned." And so, when people ask me, "How do you feel about your killer son Jason?" I say, "He's not mine!" They made a bunch of movies and said he is mine, but he is not. Look at the first movie. My son is dead.

Matt: Right. You're the psycho killer.

Betsy: No! I only killed once. Well, I mean I wiped out the whole camp, but it was only that one time. They were counselors; they should have been gone by then. I didn't kill children. I was trying to save the children.

MATT: What are your thoughts on the remakes?

BETSY: Can't say much about that because I haven't seen any of the other movies. They are just making money with those.

MATT: What is your take on being a "Scream Queen?"

BETSY: I take it as a badge of honor (laughs). I think it is so funny. First of all, I didn't try to play Mrs. Voorhees as a heavy. I never thought of her as being a killer. I never thought of her as being this terrible person. NEVER thought of her that way. I justified her to myself. You make peace over time if you have the length of a career and the years that I have been working. I'll be eighty-three the first of November, if I make it.

MATT: Up until *Friday the 13th*, you were mainly a "theater baby," as you have called yourself.

BETSY: Yes. That has always been my preference. I love doing anything live. I like standing up. I do a one-woman sort of thing where I talk about my life. I do it extemporaneously. I've always enjoyed a live audience and still do. Filmmaking was always the hurry up and waits. And it's broken up into little pieces, and I don't know. This never stimulated me. Repeating scenes over and over again to get all those different camera angles drove me crazy.

MATT: One of your early film roles was *Mister Roberts* with Henry Fonda and Jack Lemmon.

BETSY: Yes. That came after the first film. The first film was *The Long Gray Line* with Tyrone Power and Maureen O'Hara. John Ford directed it. I remember when Mr. Ford was in town doing auditions. I always called him "Mr. Ford." I still do. Mr. Ford was doing auditions in this hotel and people would go up and see him. On my audition, I walked in, and before I said anything, he said, "Okay. You're it." I said, 'Well, do you want me to read?' He said, "No. You're what I want." That's how that happened. Shortly after *The Long Gray Line* was finished, Mr. Ford wanted me for *Mister Roberts*, which was being shot in Hawaii. It was just a girls' scene with a handful of us. I was the lead gal. One day, Mr. Fonda and Mr. Ford got into a terrible squabble. Mr. Ford, when he would shoot movies, would stop drinking. When he wasn't shooting, he was a heavy drinker. He had lots and lots of friends in Hawaii, and a lot of partying began to happen. He had this beautiful yacht. One night, he invited us all for a party. He was really partying a lot, and he and Fonda just got into it. So, Mr. Ford was taken off the film. I went to see Mr. Ford soon after. They had put us up in this wonderful compound with a lot of cottages. He shared one with his wife. So, I went over to see him. He told me that the reason he was off the film was because of a gallbladder operation. I remember that he was in bed and he lifted up his pajama top to show me his bandage. He said, "See this is what I had done." But I was quite sure that wasn't the reason. They really went fists to cuffs. I'll tell you about Fonda. I liked working with him, because I was very comfortable letting him be the quiet person that he was. He was not a social person. I never felt that about him. So, I gave him his space.

MATT: You also did *Queen Bee* with Joan Crawford. Was she easy to work with?

BETSY: I got along with Joan Crawford very well. Everybody always hated her. I loved her. We stayed friends till

A classic shot of Betsy.

the end of her life. What a professional lady she was. She felt professionally about films, the way I felt about the stage. It was because of me she came on *I've Got a Secret*, and that was all live. She had never done anything on live television before. To have a crew on set is one thing, but having an audience was new to her.

MATT: Was she nervous about performing in front of a live audience?

BETSY: Yes, but *I've Got A Secret* was just a game and she sat next to our host, Garry Moore. The audience was away from the stage and the cameras were sort of blocking the audience, so she felt safe. Plus, she already had the answers. It worked out very well.

MATT: What was your take on live TV?

BETSY: When I went to New York in I think 1951 or close to 1952, everything was live. There was no tape in those days. Tape came later on. I loved live television. It was like doing theater.

MATT: Did you enjoy appearing on game shows?

BETSY: Yes. But that's another thing. I am not a game player and I've never really liked to play games. The reason was maybe because my brother was such a poor loser (laughs). How that came about was waiting for *Mister Roberts* to be released. A fellow from *I've Got a Secret* called over to the casting guy at Warner Bros. and asked if there was a celebrity in town to appear on the show. The casting agent said, "Yes, we have Betsy Palmer. We are getting ready to release *Mister Roberts*, a film she is in." Nobody knew who I was at that point. They sent me over to the show and I did it as best I knew how. Jayne Meadows was on it then, and Garry Moore, Henry Morgan, and Bill Cullen. Faye Emerson had been the second woman on the show. She was off doing a movie somewhere in Spain. So, they had me come back a few times. The sponsor, who was Winston [cigarettes], was not too happy with Faye. Faye was very political. In fact, she had been married to one of the Roosevelts' sons.

Betsy today.

Sometimes, Faye would sound off on politics and the sponsor wanted someone "safe." They never knew what Faye was going to say on the air. So, they hired me full-time thinking I was "Miss Goodie Two Shoes," the girl next door, although I have never lived next door to any girl whom I wanted to be like.

MATT: Sounds like you have had a full life.

BETSY: Yes. My life has been like that all the way down the line, and it still is.

MATT: Are you working on anything now?

BETSY: I do a lot of *Love Letters*, the play by A.R Gurney. I do it for fundraising organizations. I say, "Just get me there, put me up overnight and I'll do it for nothing." I LOVE the show and I love the character. I really do her very well, if I may say so myself. No one has really seen the show until they see me do it. I also do a lot of speaking. I talk extemporaneously for about an hour. Eventually they have to shut me up, as you can tell. I babble on and on.

MATT: I have enjoyed every minute of it. I know we must get off shortly. Is there a highlight for you in your career?

BETSY: The whole thing. I cannot have asked for more. I couldn't have planned it better. And I had a wonderful personal life. I was married to a doctor and I have a daughter. My career though has been my life.

MATT: I know you have to go and spend Mother's Day with your daughter. I thank you for taking the time to talk with me. Have a great Mother's Day.

BETSY: You're welcome, Matthew. Bye bye.

Chapter Thirteen:
DEE WALLACE

Dee Wallace is known by movie audiences as "The Quintessential Mom" for her role in the blockbuster Steven Spielberg movie *E.T. the Extra-Terrestrial.* She is also known to horror genre fans for her work in some early 1980s classics including Joe Dante's *The Howling* and Stephen King's *Cujo.* She also appeared in one of Wes Craven's first films, the gory *The Hills Have Eyes.* Since coming to Hollywood via Kansas City, Dee has not stopped working in television and films. In recent years, Dee Wallace has shared her talents teaching acting and giving "healing lessons" out of the Dee Wallace Acting Studio based in the Los Angeles area.

MATT: Can you tell me where you grew up, Dee?

DEE: I grew up in Kansas City, Kansas. I never left Kansas until I was about twenty-seven years old.

MATT: Is that when you started acting?

DEE: I started acting in Kansas City as a little girl. My mom directed all the plays at church, so I started out as baby Jesus and ended up as Mary! I have acted all my life, but not professionally till I left Kansas.

MATT: Where did you go?

DEE: I went to New York City.

MATT: What were some early roles?

DEE: I did tons of commercials and got my equity card. The first film part that I ever got was as a maid in *The Stepford Wives*. In it I had one line. That, however, is not what I consider to be the beginning of my career. One day I had made cookies and was making rounds at the studios trying to get on the lot. I finally did at Universal. That day, I met Reuben Cannon and gave him some of my cookies. While I was in his office, he got a call about this girl that was supposed to do this waitress part on TV, but she had gotten sick and couldn't do it. He covered the phone and looked at me and said, "What size do you wear?" To which I said, "What size do you need?" He sent me over and I did the first five lines on a show. That was the beginning of the beginning.

MATT: Soon you appeared in the horror film *The Hills Have Eyes*. How did you get cast in the movie?

DEE: I auditioned for it. Previously, I had done a religious film, quite an amazing part. I played a battered wife. As a result, I got in with a really good agent. The agent sent me in to audition for *The Hills Have Eyes*, and I got it.

MATT: It was one of Wes Craven's first films. What was he like as a director?

DEE: Wes is very quiet, very reserved. At least he was. That's kind of what I remember about him. It's hard to explain. He was a very quiet yet firm presence when he was on the set.

MATT: Where was the movie filmed? I have read it was in the middle of nowhere.

DEE: Oh yeah! It was out in the desert someplace. It was just far enough that it didn't fall under the Screen Actors Guild rules. Therefore, they didn't have to put us up. So, we either had to put ourselves up or drive from LA. I ultimately ended up putting myself up because it was such a far drive. It was in the middle of the desert, so we died from the heat during the day and it got very cold at night. We all had one big trailer and we all shared it, and I mean everybody! I lived a lot in my car on that set.

MATT: How long were you out there?

DEE: Probably about three weeks.

MATT: In one scene, you have a tarantula crawling on you. Was that a real tarantula?

DEE: Yes. It was a real tarantula! They all assured me tarantulas were not poisonous and that they couldn't hurt you. They were just big scary looking spiders, so somehow I got past the fear. I am not sure if I would ever do that again! But you do a lot of shit when you want your first gig.

MATT: So what we saw was a natural reaction?

DEE: I would say so. I didn't like doing that at all.

MATT: Speaking of creatures, weren't there snakes around, and at one point, snakes invaded the trailer?

DEE: I wasn't there for that. I do not know if that is a true story. It was just pretty hard working conditions as far as the weather. It was an adjustment. The bathrooms would back up. I often wondered if Elizabeth Taylor started out that way.

MATT: What was your reaction to the movie?

DEE: Holy hell, this is a violent movie! But it did what it was supposed to do. It is supposed to be a horror movie. It is supposed to be bloody and scary. If you see the remake, which was made by a lot of the same people, ours is so much scarier without the gratuitous violence.

MATT: You did a lot of television after *The Hills Have Eyes.* Can you share some of those shows with me?

DEE: I went on to do a lot of co-star and guest-starring spots. *Police Woman* was my first really big breakthrough on TV. I did a lot of TV working my way up. Another big breakthrough was also the "hooker" episode on *Lou Grant.* That was a huge breakthrough for me. It led directly to me appearing in *10* for Blake Edwards.

MATT: That is a great movie. I was going to ask you about it. How was that experience?

DEE: Blake is one of my favorite directors for whom I have ever worked. He was quintessentially old Hollywood. He knew what he wanted and he went after it. If you were professional and did your job you were "in like flint" and if you were not, you got your balls cut off. That was it. He didn't have time for people who fucked around. He and John Derek definitely were at odds about a lot of stuff. I have fond memories of Blake. I was this newbie and I had agents that didn't negotiate a dressing room for me in my contract. I didn't know any better. My first day on set, Blake came up to me and said, "Hi Dee. It's a pleasure to have you here. Is everything ok?" This was literally as I was walking onto the set. I answered, "Oh! Everything's great

Dee and co-star Dudley Moore in the film *10*.

Mr. Edwards. Everything is fine. Where's my dressing room?" He didn't miss a beat and turned around and looked at Tony Adams the producer and said, "Tony where's her dressing room?" Tony then didn't miss a beat either and said, "Uh, you know Mr. Edwards it hasn't arrived yet." And Blake said, "Well make sure it gets here for Ms. Wallace. In the meantime, put her in with Bo." Well, John Derek freaked out about that. But I will always remember Blake for never having said, "Somebody take care of the little bitch." He just stepped forward for me, and within two hours, I had a trailer. That's who he was.

MATT: Sounds like you are very grateful for that experience.

DEE: Well, after working for forty years now in the business, I really appreciate that kind of treatment. There are so many people that just don't know how to do their job. Blake was the creative person's director. It is as opposing to a lot of these guys today that know only the technical stuff. Creative stuff is not their forté. Either you get no direction today, or you get the wrong direction today.

MATT: You have worked with some big directors aside from Blake Edwards. You also worked with Steven Spielberg. Is it hard to match that sort of quality these days?

DEE: The bigger they are the more they leave you alone. They find the right person. Blake had that magical way of seeing stuff and doing things that got you where he wanted you without really directing you. For instance, he came and sat next to me right before we were getting ready to shoot the bedroom scene. He said, "Dee. What do you think about playing this nude?" The first thought was my grandma back in Kansas City. I said, 'Well Mr. Edwards, you know . . . gee, I think it's wrong for the movie. Everybody else is naked in the movie and I just tried to have sex with this guy who couldn't get it up. I don't think I would flaunt myself in front of him. Bottom line Mr. Edwards, I make my living doing commercials these days. If you give me two or three more movies, I'll take my clothes off." He looked at me and smiled and said, "Just checking." It threw me off just enough and the scene was magical. Something happened after we originally wrapped and we had to go back and shoot. They had rebuilt the set to the tune of around $100,000. As a director, Blake always watched the stuff from a monitor. He never watched you. So after a take, everybody would shut up and wait till Blake made some kind of comment after "cut." Nobody did anything till he spoke. So, here we are, they have rebuilt the expensive set, and Dudley Moore and I do the scene. Then, there is silence, and soon we hear, "I don't know who the fuck wrote it? But, we're going to print it!" Dudley and I had improvised. You couldn't work with Dudley if you didn't improvise. I was just following Dudley's lead. Blake, of course, had written it. That made it even funnier. We did it in one take and we all hear the production manager running over to Blake saying, "Blake. We spent $100,000. Let's just lay a couple down and get use of the set." Blake looked at him and said, "No. I looked at the monitor. I reviewed the monitor. I have what I want. We will not be doing it anymore." I can't tell you what it does for the entire set when you have a leader. So often you don't have a leader anymore.

MATT: You mentioned improvising with Dudley Moore. Is there anything that stands out?

DEE: There is a scene where we were really drunk, all improvised. We end up falling backwards onto the bed. It's amazing we didn't hurt ourselves. At one point, Dudley keeps pulling the sheets and I pull it back you know, stuff like that, the words said were not the words on the page. That was all improvised.

MATT: You soon did *The Howling* for Joe Dante. What did you think of Joe?

DEE: Joe and I are still friends. I think he is a brilliant director. Again he is one of those guys who are so creative that the system doesn't know what to do with them. In *The Howling* for example, all of the

Dee in a scene from *The Howling*.

cartoons were cut, which was such an ingenious part of *The Howling*. Joe wanted that and the studio wouldn't pay for it. It was important to his vision. When the reviews came out, they said how ingenious all of that stuff was. I adore Joe as a person and as a director. Just always having that sense of humor and taking care of his cast. When you feel respected and heard, you want to come forward and give it your all.

MATT: Did you like horror movies?

DEE: Truthfully?

MATT: Sure.

DEE: No. I am not a big fan of horror movies. I like suspense thrillers. I was always really scared. When I was a little girl, my older brother let me watch

King Kong. I didn't sleep for probably six months. My mother was so pissed off that she had me sleep in the room with my brother, since he let me watch it. To this day, I can't watch the *Hostel* movies or *Saw.* I am just too vulnerable emotionally.

MATT: Christopher Stone, your late husband and co-star in *The Howling*, said previously that you would take emotional baggage home with you from that day's filming. Is that true?

DEE: Yeah. I think every actor does that until they learn not to. My mother gave me some letters that I had written to her while I was shooting the movie, *10*, and I read them. I thought, *Holy hell, I didn't write these! Mary wrote these. My character wrote these.* I have since learned to let go. At some point you realize acting is what you do; it's not who I am. I don't need to act in my life. I need to be balanced and centered in my real life and flip out when they call "action."

MATT: Was *The Howling* the first movie you and Christopher did together?

DEE: Yes. Dan Black called me after I had been cast and said, "The movie is looking really great. We are just looking for the actor to play your husband. If you know anyone good looking and macho, but also he needs to have sensitivity too. Let us know." I thought, *Well duh!! I don't know why I hadn't come up with it sooner? Chris would be perfect.* I knew that psychologically if I said, "Well, my fiancé, Chris, fits that perfectly," they would have never gone for that. But I did say, "You know Dan. I worked with this actor—what's his name—Stone I think? Chris, Christopher Stone. That's right." Dan tracked him down and Chris went in and auditioned on his own and got the role. The next day, Dan calls the house. I answered the phone. Dan said, "Dee?" I said, "Yeah." He said, "I am sorry. I must have dialed the wrong number. I am trying to find Christopher Stone. He came in and was great." I said, "No, Dan you dialed the right number." Then, there was a pause, and he said, "Oh shit!" I said, "If I told you we were engaged, would you have had him in?" Dan said, "Hell no." I said, "The good news is you will only have to get one trailer." We all become very good friends and went on to do *Cujo* together.

MATT: Was it hard watching Christopher do the love scene by the fire in *The Howling*?

DEE: I didn't watch him do the love scene. I went into town and got drunk. Actually Joe came up to me a few days before filming that scene and said, "So Dee, are you planning on being on the set when we shoot this?" I looked at him and said, "You don't want me here do you?" He said, "I think it might make everybody uncomfortable, not so much with Elisabeth Brooks [who I do not even want to discuss] but mostly the crew because they really care about you." Well that's all he had to say. He played me so well. I said to him, "I think you're right. Find somebody to take me to dinner Joe." So, I went to town and got drunk. I was in bed when Chris walked in. I said, "So, how did it go?" He said, "It was 32 degrees. I froze my balls off. She had bad breath and droopy breasts. Go to bed." And that was the end of the discussion.

MATT: He sounds like a special person.

DEE: He was my soul mate.

MATT: One of your co-stars in the movie was character actor John Carradine, who was in many Universal horror films back in the day. What was John like to work with?

DEE: John was a dear, dear man and was ridden with arthritis and yet he never complained one moment. It was freezing cold the night he had to work by the fire. He was an absolute total professional like most of the older gentlemen were taught to be. He shared some stories with us. We got to work with a lot of icons in that film. Again, that was Joe Dante's idea.

MATT: There were a lot of classic horror references throughout the movie. Aside from the constant "wolf" references, did you spot up any?

DEE: If you go back to the movie, there are a lot of characters that got their names from a lot of the older horror movie actors and characters. That was all Joe's idea.

MATT: In one scene, you're watching Robert Picardo's character morph into a wolf. Were you acting to anything?

DEE: No. I was hearing Joe's voice, "Ok. Now his ears are growing. Here comes his nose. Now, he is getting taller." Finally, I had it, and I said, "Joe. Just tell me what sequence it happens in and I will do it myself." I just had to go to La La Land myself, and every time Joe's voice came in, it kind of broke that for me. So, I just learned the sequence of things and did it myself. They put Picardo in weeks later.

MATT: Did you get asked to appear in any of the sequels?

DEE: They sent me the script for the second one and I said, "Thanks. Don't do porn yet."

MATT: You did an interview maybe about twenty years ago. In the interview, you said that *The Howling* had been one of the best experiences of your life. Does that still hold true all this time later?

DEE: Absolutely, absolutely. I would have to say I loved my experience on *10*, but everything with *The Howling* was wonderful, from being engaged to Chris and working with him. Of course, having the lead and having a director that encouraged me. We just had a great time. I have extremely fond memories of doing *The Howling*. *Cujo* was a freaking nightmare to shoot, and it's my favorite thing I ever did.

MATT: Why is that? Did you not want to do another horror movie?

DEE: *Cujo* was a tour de force. I never really looked at it as a horror movie. I look at it as a physiological film. It was a psychological battle. I don't consider it a horror movie.

MATT: Had you read the book?

DEE: Nope and I didn't read it after I got the part.

MATT: Did you meet Stephen King?

DEE: I did and I really like him. I don't know if it's still there, but on his web site, he said that *Cujo* was his favorite book ever brought to the big screen. He thought I should have won an Academy Award for my performance.

Dee in a scene from *Cujo*.

MATT: Didn't they use several dogs throughout the movie?

DEE: Yes. There were five of them, all trained to go after
             different toys. We had to tie their tails down with
             fish wire because they were wagging them all the
             time.

MATT: And a robot dog too, right?

DEE: I don't think we ever used that one much. The
             stunt man did use it during the big attack scene
             and he rammed his head against the car when Cujo
             rams the car. If you wouldn't ask a man to do that,
             you wouldn't ask an animal to do that. The real
             dogs did everything else.

MATT: Was it hard working with so many dogs?

DEE: No. It was easier with them being present. At the beginning, production just wanted to use the dogs for their stuff and not use us with the dogs. We learned very quickly that neither Danny Pintauro, nor I were reacting the same way without the real dogs being there. It's easy to cross over into really believing they were dangerous when you were acting with them.

MATT: Were you ever scared in real life during the shoot?

DEE: Oh yeah! Part of you says, "Holy hell. I'm scared." When they drugged the dog and put the dog on top of me and he wasn't quite out yet, I said, "All right, you guys, he's not going to come back, right? He's not going to wake up lying on top of me?" I was gone; that was it for me. The whole thing was grueling and emotionally exhausting. I pushed myself further than I could ever have pushed myself. It really is the thing I'm proud of.

MATT: How long were you in that car shooting?

DEE: It was about six or seven weeks.

MATT: How old was Danny Pintauro, who played your son?

DEE: He was about six. He was bar none the best child actor I have ever worked with. And I have worked with some really brilliant ones. Simply because the ranges of emotions he had to play. He had so much more than most kids that I have worked with. Of course, all the kids in *E.T.* were obviously brilliant. But Danny and I just had to create this amazing bond. We were in every scene together.

MATT: Did he really bite you at one point? I read that somewhere?

Dee:

No he didn't.

Matt:

Wasn't it cold in the car?

Dee:

Heaters were brought in at my request. It was freezing and it was raining most of the time too. They had to hook up heaters in the front of the Pinto because we were just freezing to death.

Matt:

Do you have a personal favorite memory from *Cujo*?

Dee:

I do, but it isn't from filming the picture. One day, Chris and I were driving to the set, which was on this big farm. We were running late and I was barely going to make it on time. We turned a corner in the road and there is a whole herd of sheep standing in the middle of the road blocking us from going. They were looking directly at us. Chris stopped the car and we both sat there for a minute. All of a sudden, in this character voice Chris says, "Ok you guys. Get out and give me all your sweaters!" I swear we must have sat there and laughed for ten minutes. They wouldn't move with the horn. Finally, we had to get out and shoo them away. Isn't it funny the stuff you remember? That was one of the fun moments of shooting *Cujo*; well, there weren't many fun moments. Another fun memory was Gary, the stunt guy, when he would be in his dog suit and I would be getting ready for this heavy scene and he would say, "Dee, Dee." I would look over and he would lift his leg and pretend like he was peeing on the Pinto. Stuff like that. We tried to keep ourselves entertained.

Matt:

What do you think makes the movie hold up all these years?

DEE: It's good. I think women can identify with saving their kid. There's this whole story about the adults trying to find out how to be happy and complete in their relationships. It's about fear, whether you know it or not, when you watch it. You understand you're watching a part of yourself that's struggling with another part of yourself and trying to stay safe. It's a universal theme.

MATT: You did *E.T.* for Steven Spielberg. How did you get involved with the movie?

DEE: I auditioned for Steven's movie *Used Cars*, which thankfully I did not get. But he remembered me, and when *E.T.* came along, he just offered me the part in the movie.

MATT: Of all things you have appeared in, I think it's safe to say *E.T.* had the most universal appeal and popularity. What's it like to be part of such a groundbreaking movie?

DEE: Well, it's my *Wizard of Oz*. Anytime I walk onto a stage, they are going to play the theme from *E.T.* Mostly I'm thrilled that I am involved in a film that touched so many hearts and it still does.

MATT: Did you ever worry about being labeled a "Scream Queen?"

DEE: I am labeled as a "Scream Queen." I'm labeled as the "most quintessential mom." Let me tell you. Ask Angelina Jolie: if we worried about everything people said about us, we would be dead. Actors want to act, period. They want to emote. They want to touch you. They want to use their instrument and they use it whenever they can wherever they

A recent portrait of Dee.

can within the realms of what is morally okay with them.

MATT: Speaking of acting, you currently teach acting, don't you?

DEE: I did teach acting for twelve years. I had one of the largest studios out here in L.A. I do private lessons sometimes.

MATT: What made you want to teach acting?

DEE: I am a great teacher. I taught high school. Then, it became the passion of my life for twelve years. Then three years ago, I said, "You know, it's time for me to move on. It's time to do me again." My real passion is the healing work that I do now. I have a couple of books out on the subject. I also do private healing sessions and seminars.

MATT: What kind of healing in case people are curious?

DEE: Energetic healing. It's all about directing your own energy to create what you want. It's a more proactive approach to letting the universe unfold. You have to direct your energy. You are the god energy. It's about taking responsibility for your own life. Do you want to be unhappy? Do you want to be unhealthy? If you don't, then what do you want?

MATT: When did you start doing healing?

DEE: About ten years ago. A lot of it was developed in the studio. It's branched out exponentially now into private lessons and teaching. As I said, I have a couple of books out on the subject and a couple of radio shows that have nice followings.

MATT: Sounds like these days you are keeping busy. What is currently in the works?

DEE: I have a lot of stuff coming out. *Bonnie and Clyde* has been pushed back. I'm not sure when we are doing that. Another movie I was supposed to start tomorrow has now been pushed back because of the economic situation.

MATT: You recently did the remake of *Halloween* with Rob Zombie. Did you like that?

DEE: I freaking love Rob Zombie. I love him! I think he is going to be one of our biggest directors. I hope he gets out and does some stuff other than the horror genre. He loves you to improve, loves for you to be in the moment, and loves you to bring in your own ideas. He is not like his persona at all. He's got a genius about him.

MATT: I know you have to go, Dee. Thank you so much for taking the time to speak with me.

DEE: You're welcome.

Chapter Fourteen:
P.J. SOLES

Every year when Halloween rolls around, there's one face you can count on seeing across millions of television screens across the world. That face belongs to the ever spunky P. J. Soles. P. J. is as Halloween as "trick or treating." Both *Halloween* and *Carrie* have been voted two of the most popular films to be seen on Hallows Eve. Aside from her roles in two of the most popular horror films ever, she also appeared in some of the best-loved comedies of the early 1980s including *Stripes* with Bill Murray and *Private Benjamin* with Goldie Hawn. Starring with punk rock pioneers, The Ramones, in *Rock 'n' Roll High School* also cemented P. J.'s status with a generation, and it seems every generation has since followed. One of P. J.'s most famous lines from *Halloween* is, "See anything you like?" And P. J. fans would like to answer quite simply, "Yes, we do . . . you." Below is my interview with this "Halloween Gal."

MATT: P.J., where were you born?

P.J.:   I was born in Frankfurt, Germany. My mother was from Englewood, New Jersey. My dad was from Holland. My parents met in Germany after my mother's first husband was killed the last day of World War II. She went to see where he was buried after being killed. In those days, they asked the family if they wanted to have their soldier sent back home or buried where they died. The family opted for him to stay there, and she went to see where he was buried. My dad had been working for the Dutch underground when he was captured and spent eleven months in a Nazi work camp. George Patton helped free his camp and brought them to the same Army base where my mother was staying. They met after a couple of weeks at a dance on the same base. So, thank goodness it all happened! They had to go through a lot to get me.

MATT: Sounds like it! You moved around quite a bit when you were young, right?

P.J.: Yeah. Both my parents stayed in Germany after they met. My mother was the first to get a job because she was an American. She worked for the head of a new company called AIU, which has since become AIG. It started as American International Underwriters and it was an insurance company for American soldiers and American companies overseas. Since my dad spoke six languages, my mom got him a job, and he eventually worked his way up to representing the company and helping them branch out around the world. We moved from Frankfurt, Germany, to Morocco, to Casablanca, and then we moved to Maracaibo, Venezuela, with a short stop in Oakland, New Jersey. Then, we moved to Brussels, Belgium, and I came back when I was eighteen to go to college in New York State.

MATT: What did you study in college?

P.J.: When I was in high school, I was editor of my school paper for two years. I took it very seriously and thought I was going to be working for a magazine or become a writer. I spoke French and Spanish. When I went to college, my major was Russian. For my senior high school class trip, we went to Russia and I just felt that Russia was going to be a country that the US was going to be dealing with in the future, and I wanted to be a part of it. I was pretty serious, but all along, I had been in the school plays in all those countries I lived in. It was something I just did for fun, like playing basketball. It just never occurred to me to do it seriously. I didn't know you could make a living doing that. When I graduated college, I was going to start off by being an interpreter at the U.N. and work my way into something. At the same time, I was toying with the idea of working at a magazine, but my roommate was from New York City, and every weekend we would go and have a lot of fun. Then, the summer between my freshman and sophomore year that's when I discovered the Actors Studio, and I went, "Wow! You could do this for a living. It's not just for fun." Soon, I met a guy, Joshua White, who became my boyfriend and he suggested that I meet with an agent. His sister was an actress. He took me to the Lester Lewis Agency and they signed me that day. They sent me out for work the next day. I got the first commercial I ever went up for and that was Crisco. I started making really good money. Meanwhile, I was transferring from Briarcliff College to Georgetown University in D.C.; I was one of two girls picked for their foreign-language school. I went for a couple of months and I was lonely. I had already made friends in New York City that summer, I had a boyfriend, and I had an agent. New York City was calling. I finally decided to move back to the city. My parents were living in Istanbul, Turkey, at that time, and the communications weren't what they are today. It took them till June to realize I wasn't attending college! I kind of always felt bad about that, but I didn't want to hurt them.

MATT: What did they think of it?

P.J.:   At first, they weren't happy at all. We are talking 1969-1970. It was wild in the city, a lot was going on. I wasn't one of the crazy wild people, but I definitely hung out with hippies, musicians, and artists, which was fun. My parents just didn't think it was a great move on my part. Then, they saw the Crisco oil commercial on TV and went, "Oh, my god, Pamela! Look!" Then, they got all excited and supportive.

MATT: What was the city like in those days?

P.J.:   We were carefree and it was wild. I went to Woodstock with my first boyfriend, the one that I met at the Actors Studio. He did The Joshua Light Show from the Fillmore East for the first couple of days at Woodstock until it got too rainy and the wind blew the screen down. But we were there and we were brought in by helicopter every day. After that, I met a guy named Steven Soles, who would become my first husband. I was always going to recording studios and hanging out with people playing music. I watched James Taylor play music, hung out at CBGB's, went to Chinatown at three o'clock in the morning. The whole thing was great. Just jump in a cab go uptown go downtown nothing like Los Angeles where everything closes at nine p.m. here!

MATT: What were some early acting roles you got while in New York?

P.J.:   It was a lot of commercials. I was tall and fresh-faced and I looked like I was from California, and yet I could act. I had a good career going. I was a pretty girl who could speak! People have adjusted to the fact that some models do have brains. I also got a job for a year on a soap opera,

Love Is a Many Splendored Thing. That was valuable for my training, helped me learn about cameras, and blocking etc. It was also good since it was being filmed two blocks from my house.

Matt: One of your first projects was a television movie called *Blood Bath.* Do you remember that?

P.J.: I really have few memories of that. The guy who made it sent me a copy of it recently. I remember it when I see it. In the film, I was in bed and in my PJs and I screamed. That was my first scream on screen! I was good at screaming! It was filmed in New York, but I don't remember filming it or where we shot it exactly. It's kind of weird; I don't know why I blanked it out.

Matt: What made you move out west?

P.J.: Everyone kept saying, "If you want to do movies, you got to move to California." I had some friends that had already done it. I knew I wasn't really into the Broadway scene. I didn't drink, I wasn't a smoker, I didn't stay up late, I was always falling asleep by eleven o'clock. That kind of lifestyle wasn't for me. I was more suited for the film life.

Matt: It wasn't before long that you got cast in *Carrie.* How did you get involved with the film?

P.J.: That was when I first came to Los Angeles in 1975. I remember it was probably October or early November, when George Lucas and Brian De Palma had a famous joint casting session. George was looking for *Star Wars* people, and Brian was looking for people to put in *Carrie.* They both sat behind the same desk and they saw, it seemed, every teenager in town! I remember waiting in line

P.J. during the filming of *Carrie*.

for like two hours sitting in the hallway. Basically, I just walked in and they both looked at me and Brian said, "I will put her on my list," and George went, "Okay." As I turned to leave, Brian said, "For your next callback, wear your hat." I was wearing that red baseball hat. When I went for the audition, I didn't want to go for the pretty girl look. I wanted to go for the funky, tomboy look. I wore overalls and a striped shirt and braids, pretty much how I looked in the movie. I think there were three or four callbacks and then a screen test; every time, though, Brian would say, "Bring your hat." Finally, after the screen test, I got the part. Most of us girls who ended up screen testing for Brian got a part, maybe just not the part we tested for! I actually tested for the Nancy Allen part and Nancy Allen really wanted the Sissy Spacek part. Amy Irving also wanted the Sissy Spacek part. Brian didn't think Sissy Spacek would get the part. However, Jack Fisk, who was the set designer, was her husband, and he said to Brian, "Please test my wife. She is really great." Of course, she ended up blowing them all away. So, she got the part of Carrie. Amy got her part, Nancy got her part, and I got the part of Norma, who in the script has only one line in the beginning at the volleyball game when I say, "Thanks a lot, Carrie," and that was it. But Brian kept me on after seeing the dailies from that day. When I took off my hat and I whacked Sissy on the head, one of my pins got caught in her hair and I just yanked it out and everyone died laughing, and so Brian said to me, "We are going to keep you on for the next six weeks." He put me in all those other scenes. Norma was not in the script. I was very thankful for that. It was all because of that hat!

MATT: What was he like as a new director?

P.J.: He was good in that he could completely visualize the entire movie in his head. When we went over the movie during one of the three callbacks, we were at his apartment. His dining room was completely covered with storyboards of every scene, every shot. I was amazed. I didn't realize that's how directors work. He literally had every scene pretty much drawn-out as to how he could shoot it. He was confident and visualized ahead of time what he wanted, and as he assembled his players, he sat in his chair and watched it unfold. Of course, he was always delighted if you asked something, which my character had to. I was the best at improvisation next to Nancy, most of the time. Brian would let you know he liked something by smiling after the take and moving on. If he got what he wanted visually, even if it was uncomfortable for the actors, he would be satisfied and move forward.

MATT: Was Stephen King involved with the production at all? Was he ever watching what was going on?

P.J.: He was there the first day. There was some kind of ruckus he got involved in, and then later, I overheard someone say, "The writer is banned from the set." I just remembered thinking, *Wow. How could you do that? That's so unfair.* I was so naïve. Steven Spielberg would show up all the time. He was not known at that point, but he proceeded to ask all the girls out one by one. He went down the whole line, and we all said no, except for Amy Irving, who said yes.

MATT: Did you know how you were going to be killed off in the movie?

P.J.: No. That's an interesting question because nobody knew. In the script, all it said about the prom killing scene was something like, "Then Betty Buckley's character dies, and Nancy Allen's character dies." It was my job to pick up Betty Buckley every morning at her hotel. Betty had been an old girlfriend of Brian's in New York; that's how she got the part. She was staying at the Chateau Marmont on Sunset Boulevard in Hollywood. She didn't have a driver's license since she was a New Yorker and didn't own a car. I had a little blue truck, and Brian asked me to pick her up every morning. I don't know why; I guess he was trying to give her a friend since she was all alone from New York. She was the funniest. I would pick her up and she would be putting on her makeup at six a.m. while on the way to set. I would say to her, "What are you doing? There are makeup people waiting for us." She said, "I'm not going to walk onto the soundstage looking like this. Brian might see me." She was so funny. The day she was to film her death scene, the whole ride there she was so nervous. I asked "What's the matter?" She said, "I don't know, but he is going to have something horrendous planned for me. What if it doesn't go right? What if I don't have a stunt woman? We ended kind of on a bad note as boyfriend and girlfriend." I said "He must like you. He gave you the part." She said, "He probably did it on purpose just so he could do this death scene." It was this whole crazy thing. Of course, she had a stunt double and she was fine. As far as mine goes, it was only last-minute that they wanted to use the fire hose to kill me. The fire chief that was manning the hose said, "We can't put this near anybody safely," cause Brian really wanted to whack my head around. So, Nick, the stuntman, said, "Well, I will hold the hose." They put it on full force and I never felt anything so strong. It threw my head around and it went full force in my ear and broke my eardrum. The pain was excruciating. I just slid and slithered down on the floor. Once you break your eardrum, you lose your equilibrium. The two grips came running and they grabbed me and brought me to my dressing room. Oh my god, the pain was just so excruciating. They took me to the hospital, I was off balance for a couple of days, but

for six months, I had trouble hearing. It healed
fine; I was okay overall. I didn't know it was going
to be that bad though. If I had known, I would
have said, "Wait a minute." That was the actual
shot they used in the movie. That was all real
footage of someone getting hurt!

MATT: So, you were never knocked unconscious as I have
read before?

P.J.: I wasn't unconscious. I do remember feeling sort
of woozy and losing my balance up against the
bleachers. I literally slid down. I didn't get knocked
unconscious or black out, but I just lost my bearings!
Ouch!

MATT: How long did it take to shoot the prom scene?

P.J.: The prom sequence took at least two weeks; it
could have been longer. I think there was a
Thanksgiving break somewhere in there, or maybe
Christmas . . . not sure exactly. I remember we left
and came back. It was awesome: every day we were
going to the prom! It was kind of cool.

MATT: What did you think when you were watching Sissy
Spacek acting possessed on stage?

P.J.: (Lets out a big laugh) Ha ha! It was so funny! It
was awesome. You know you're filming, and it's
something you know is going to happen but still
gets you. I just remember thinking that her reaction
was unbelievable. She was so great: she really, really
looked scary. She *was* Carrie. I remember they
had to do a couple of days after that and she had a
trailer parked outside the back of the studio in
Culver City. She didn't want to have to wash off
the blood and rematch it and all that. So, she slept

a couple of nights with that blood on her, using a plastic sheet on her bed. That's commitment!

MATT: Didn't she also insist on being buried in the second to last scene and having her own hand come out of the grave grabbing Amy Irving's character?

P.J.: Yes. I remember that very much because, like I said, her husband, Jack Fisk, was the set designer. He built this little box, and he was going to have an animatronic hand come out of it. Sissy was like, "No, no. You build something and you put oxygen in there and I'm getting in the box. It's going to be my hand." I was like, *Whoa, even I wouldn't do that.* That would be kind of scary. She was pretty much underground. But she wanted it to be as real as possible and totally insisted that it be her hand. I thought that was cool.

MATT: What was she like when not filming?

P.J.: You know, when we met at the screen test, she was really darling. At the beginning of filming, she introduced herself and let us know that she wanted to hang out and have fun, but she really needed to concentrate and she needed to feel the alienation from everybody. She wanted us all to know it was intentional, but it wasn't because she didn't like us. She just needed to feel alienated from us. Towards the end, she became friendly with everybody. She and I got along well. We were friendly afterwards and got together a couple of times. She was a really nice girl.

MATT: What did you think of the movie when you first saw it?

P.J.: I was really stunned. I was very surprised. I wasn't

quite sure how it would all fit together. I had seen the dailies all along. Brian invited us to the screening room every night after filming to watch them. That was another nice thing that most directors do not do. They almost never let you see dailies, certainly not a ruckus, rowdy bunch like us. John Travolta was there all the time howling and Brian is sitting in the back with his assistant, Martin, jotting down notes, but all of us were just having a great time. I don't know how he could have concentrated. In any event, when I saw it for the first time, I thought it was a really beautiful film considering the subject matter. It had a lot of good emotions. Of course, Piper Laurie brought such class and such reality to it and coupled with Sissy, if it hadn't been for those two I think it would have been a completely different movie. They just really made it a film.

MATT: Soon after *Carrie*, you were cast in *Halloween*. Is it true John Carpenter had you in mind for the role of Lynda?

P.J.: That's what I have heard afterwards. I read a bunch of interviews. He didn't tell me that at the time. I auditioned like everybody else and I read a couple of scenes for John. Afterwards, he said, "Wow! You're the only one who has read *totally* right." And later, he said, "Well that's why you got the part." After I got the part, he said, "Can you stay and help me pick out your boyfriend?" So, I stayed, and there were three guys up for the part of Bob, and I picked John Michael Graham. Originally, they were hoping to get Dennis Quaid. At the time, I was married to him. Debra Hill was hoping she could get him. When they told me the dates they would be shooting the scenes of Bob and Lynda, I made a quick call to Dennis, but he was

P.J. on the set of *Halloween* with director John Carpenter.

working on a TV movie at the time. The timing just didn't work for him.

MATT: That would have been interesting.

P.J.: It would have been fun!

MATT: What did you think when you first read the script?

P.J.: I really liked the girls. I thought that we all had vast differences in our personalities and characters. I loved my part. I thought I had the best role. During filming, Jamie was always telling me that it was unfair that I got to play Lynda and not her because I was the one that had the most fun. I told her she was the lead. She said, "It doesn't matter.

I'm the boring lead. You get to have all the fun and you get the cute scenes." I never heard the end of it (laughs). I liked the story. I liked it because it was so simple. I was excited about my part. After *Carrie*, it was like a huge part. I only had that one line in *Carrie* and I made a lot out of it and I was determined to do the same for here.

MATT: Were there that many "totallys" in the script?

P.J.: I added more. In fact, I said to John Carpenter, "I'm going to push this. Every time I can say it, I'm going to say totally, so if you need to pull me back, if it's over the top, tell me." I think maybe only once he told me to curb them. I forget the scene and how many times I said it. There's probably an outtake of it somewhere.

MATT: Was there a final count of how many times you said "totally?"

P.J.: People come up to me and tell me all the time, but I don't remember the number (laughs).

MATT: What was Jamie Lee Curtis like? It was one of her first films.

P.J.: She was certainly a lot of fun and the opposite of Laurie Strode. It was her first movie and she was so excited. She was nineteen and she was just having a blast. She always made sure she was doing a great job. There wasn't a lot of time to pal around because it was a short schedule. We were just moving really quickly, one or two takes and next, next, next. Time was of the essence. Most of the time, we hung out was at lunch or in the trailer when other people were filming their stuff. We still send each other Christmas cards every year!

P.J. pictured with *Halloween* co-stars Jamie Lee Curtis and Nancy Kyes.

MATT: In one scene, you got topless. Did you have any issues about that?

P.J.:   Yes. In *Carrie*, during the shower scene, I had the towel on. I was the only one with a towel around me. With my parents in mind, I was like, "I'm not taking off anything." I guess the other girls wanted to show off their goods. I told Brian, "No. I'm sorry. My parents are going to see this." But in *Halloween*, again, it wasn't in the script. In the script, it was just "Bob and Lynda go upstairs," and that's all that was written. Then, John had the idea of The Shape (Michael Myers) coming back upstairs and blah, blah, blah. It was not decided yet how I was going to die and all that. John said, "When Bob goes downstairs and comes back up, can you do something to kind of tease Bob? Or

P.J. with co-stars Jamie Lee Curtis and Nancy Kyes during the filming of *Halloween*.

who you think is Bob under the sheet, but is really Michael Myers. If you don't feel comfortable, it's okay, whatever you want to do. Maybe you can give a little flash?" They wanted to make it very sexy, but it wasn't pre-arranged. I said, "Yes. I think I can come up with something. Why don't you just roll camera and we will do it." I had a nail file in my bag, so when he came back up, I was filing my nails, and I said, "See anything you like?" That just came off the top of my head. It happened quickly. I thought my parents won't notice. But of course they did! (Laughs). They had taken a couple of friends with them to see it, and they said, "You could have at least warned us."

MATT: When you were filming your death scene were you scared at all?

P.J.:   No. It's not scary in any way. It's hard to make it look real. Nick Castle was The Shape under the sheet during my death scene, and he was so afraid of hurting me that he barely brushed the cord against my neck. I was like, "Nick, I have to die here! Could you use a little pressure?" He said, "I don't want to hurt you or make you black and blue." I said, "It's okay. I just need something." So, we did it again and still nothing. I said, "Pull it again harder. I need to choke. You're killing me here; you can't be tickling me. I'm not that good an actress." He was just so sweet and he didn't want to hurt me in any way. From that scene, I always remember thinking, *Oh my god. This is the last time they're going to see me on camera so I need to extend my scene.* That's why you hear me choking all the way out of frame. I wanted the camera to be on for a really long time. I just kept going, "Uuhgghgghhgg (making choking noises). I'm not dead yet. Don't say cut!" I didn't realize then I would be stuffed in the closet. So I did have one last shot to do.

MATT: Who exactly was The Shape? I know you mentioned Nick Castle, but weren't Tony Moran and Tommy Wallace also Michael Myers? Can you clarify that for me?

P.J.:   Tony Moran was just in the very last scene when The Shape takes off the mask. Tony was only cast for that scene. He goes to all the conventions and says he's the Mike Myers of the original *Halloween*. But he was really cast for his face; they wanted somebody good-looking. For the whole movie, it was mostly Tommy Wallace and Nick Castle who would fill in. Whoever was available that day and not doing something else would put on the mask and overalls.

MATT: Did you ever see any of the remakes?

P.J.:   I was invited to the *H2O* movie premiere by Jamie Curtis. I remember as I was watching the opening credits I thought, *They could have had some flash backs of Laurie dreaming about what it would have been like if Annie and Lynda had grown older with her. What would they be like now?* And then she would have woken up. I thought that would have been really cool. They didn't think of that though.

MATT: Someone should tell Rob Zombie and he could do it for his next *Halloween*.

P.J.:   Well, I would have liked to have been in the first or the second of Rob Zombie's. I gave him my original script from *Halloween*, my original with all my notes. I gave it to him for his fortieth birthday and that was way before he was signed on to do the re-imaginings. Not that I gave it to him in the hopes of getting another part, or that I ever thought he would have anything to do with *Halloween*. He told me *Halloween* was the movie that made him want to become a director. I couldn't think of anything else to give him. He called me the next day and said, "It's the best birthday present I have ever got. It's going in my vault and the only hands that will ever touch it are mine. I will cherish it forever." So, I gave it to the right person. My kids would have sold it at a garage sale.

MATT: After *Halloween*, you did *Rock 'n' Roll High School* with The Ramones. What was that experience like?

P.J.:   It was awesome. It was one of my favorite times. I was determined to bring as much energy to that part as possible. It was a hard fought battle to get the part because every girl in town was up for it.

Rosanna Arquette really wanted it. I probably had to go back six times and meet with the director Alan Arkush and Michael Finnell and Roger Corman who were producing it. Roger Corman told me to make my hair more blonde and I would get the part. That's the only thing he ever said to me.

MATT: Looks like it must have been a blast making that?

P.J.: Every day was so much fun! Arkush had so much spunk and energy he finally got to make a movie, even though it was such a tight budget and it was only a twenty-one day shooting schedule, it was a lot of excitement in the air. It was really fun.

MATT: Were you a punk rock chick?

P.J.: No! (Laughs). It was something I kind of invented for myself. I had only $200 for wardrobe. Deborah Nadoolman, who was married to John Landis, was my wardrobe girl. She came to my house one day with a couple of things. I said, "These things are horrible. I'm going to go buy my own wardrobe." At that time, there was a store in Beverley Hills that had come from New York City. I went there and literally spent my whole salary on my wardrobe. But it made the part. I even got the red sunglasses with the lightning bolts there.

MATT: What was it like working with the band?

P.J.: Working with The Ramones was great. I had not heard of them before the movie. People always ask me about them. Allan Arkush gave me a cassette of The Ramones and said, "Go home and listen to this. Remember you are their #1 fan." I went home and put the tape in. I was married to Dennis at the time, and we were both looking at each other thinking, *This is music? How can I play their #1 fan?* Little by little, it grew on me, and certainly now, I love their music. I love, love, love it. Actually just last Saturday night I went to a Ramones tribute. I go every year. It's done at the Hollywood Forever Cemetery. All the proceeds go to cancer research. Johnny died from prostate cancer and Joey had lymphoma. Joey is buried in New York but Johnny and Dee Dee are both buried at the Hollywood Forever Cemetery. They invite everyone in and we sit on the headstones. You could bring your family, a picnic basket, beer, wine, blankets. They used to screen the movies up against the mausoleum wall; now, they have a screen.

MATT: Weren't you also hurt during the filming of *Rock 'n' Roll High School*?

P.J.: I didn't really get hurt. I just got stepped on and pushed around a lot. The concert scenes were filmed at the Roxy in Los Angeles. Production had put a notice out that there was going to be a Ramones concert and we needed an audience. These were hardcore punk rock fans. They came to watch a concert not watch a concert being filmed. So, when we filmed, we would have to stop and start and stop and start. You're not just going to get The Ramones playing twelve songs in a row. So, the fans were very annoyed and they didn't understand that I had to come down and get in the front. They were just always pushing me out of the way. The director kept announcing over the megaphone "Please let the actors do their work! We are filming them. They have to get to the front!" A couple of times we stopped because I would literally just get pushed out of the crowd.

MATT: Is there a remake of that currently in the works?

P.J.:   How can they do that without The Ramones? How could you duplicate The Ramones? I don't know. Why touch that movie? They could use the title and maybe make *Rock 'n' Roll College* (laughs). There's something so perfect and endearing about that movie and The Ramones that I just don't think they could get that today.

MATT: Right after that, you did *Private Benjamin* with Goldie Hawn.

P.J.:   Let's see. Was that before or after *Stripes*?

MATT: I think it was before.

P.J.:   Yes. I wore the same uniform in both movies. They had put my name on my army greens and my boots. When I did *Stripes*, they had my uniform, and they said, "Oh. This uniform has your name in it." I was just hoping it would still fit! (Laughs). *Private Benjamin* again was an audition situation. There were a lot of parts in that one. There was a different director for the movie at first. He hired us girls and we were all ready to go and suddenly Goldie Hawn, who was the producer also, changed the director. She also wanted to have a new casting session. I was just so infuriated. I said to my agent, "Come on, that's so unfair. A new director? A new cast? Can't you get me in there?" She called and called to no avail. She did say they are holding auditions for Wanda Winter on such and such date and time. I found out Goldie did not want to hire any other blondes. So I got a black wig, put my hair up, I got glasses, and I was kind of going into the audition in disguise. I was going to try and fool them. It was funny because I went to the casting session thinking I would break in. If you're not on the list they don't just see you. Still I went anyway. There was only one other girl sitting on the couch and I said to the receptionist, "I am here to audition for Wanda Winter." She said, "What's your name?" I said, "P. J. Soles." She said, "You are not on the list." Then the girl on the couch said, "You're not P. J. Soles. Why are you saying you're P. J. Soles? I know P. J. Soles, and you're not her." I was like "Shhhhhhhhh." I begged with the receptionist. I told her I really wanted to audition for the part. I told her my agent told me to show up here, which was not true. She gets on the phone and she goes, "There's an actress out here who really wants to be seen for the part. I guess maybe you should see her because she's really a bitch." That's what the receptionist said! I went in and I read the scene and Goldie was there, and they liked me a lot. At the end, I took off my wig and I said, "I had this part before and I still want it." They were happy I did that and they gave me the part. Goldie was like, "You have to wear the wig." She was smart she wanted to be the blonde. As you see, there is no other blonde in the movie. Well, there is Craig T. Nelson, but he doesn't have enough hair to qualify.

MATT: The next year, you did *Stripes* with Bill Murray. What was he like to work with?

P.J.: (Laughs) Bill is like a roller coaster ride. He keeps you on your toes. I did improvisation starting with *Carrie.* I always tried adding something to my characters. So, with *Stripes*, it was awesome because Bill came from Second City and *Saturday Night Live,* and improvisation is their thing. So, here I was working with a master of improvisation. He just had to set it up and I just went along on the ride, especially the scene in the kitchen. That was shot at three in the morning. In the script it said, "We are on a hill watching fireworks, etc." The scene was just about us getting to that kiss. We didn't have a lot of time for that, so I said, "Let's just do it in the kitchen." We walk in to the kitchen and they bring in the cameras. Bill opens up the refrigerator and pulls out a carrot and I said, "What are you going to do with that?" And Ivan Reitman, the director goes, "Wait, wait. Let's just roll it." What you saw was pretty much all one and two takes. I just followed Bill's lead. It was so exciting.

MATT: It seemed at your peak you decided to turn away from your acting career and have a family?

P.J.: Right. Dennis and I got divorced. I had met a pilot. He had given me his number and said "If you ever get divorced from Dennis, give me a call. I'll take you for a P-51 Mustang ride." Flying was in the family. My father had an airplane. My brother was a pilot and died in a private plane crash right before I did *Rock 'n' Roll High School.* Flying was always part of our family. When Dennis and I got divorced right after Christmas, I said to myself, *I don't know. I guess I'll give him a call.* We fell in love immediately. I got that P-51 ride. I had a son, named him Sky. Then I had a daughter, Ashley. After I gave birth to my son, it just seemed very hard to juggle doing films and being a mother. I did a couple of TV shows. I wanted to stick closer to home. I tried avoiding going on location. I did go out to Virginia to film *Sweet Dreams* with Ed Harris and that was really awesome. In those days, if you were an actress and they knew you were married and you had a child, you lost your starlet appeal. It's a whole game they play, whatever. Once I had my second child, it got even harder.

MATT: Lately, you have been appearing a lot more in movies and looks like you're keeping real busy. What are you up to?

P.J.: Yeah! Kids grow up! My son is twenty-five years old. He is the captain of his own Coast Guard cutter in Key West. He has done well for himself. Captain of your own ship at twenty-five is awesome. My daughter has one more year to go in college. She is an English major and songwriter. She has two bands. I have always written songs, and my current boyfriend and I have been writing country songs. I have been focusing on that a lot. People are always kicking me about writing an autobiography. So, I started doing that. Hopefully, I will have a book out one of these days, too! Also, you said I have been working lately in films. That's because of the fact that these movies I did, movies like *Halloween* and *Carrie*, have held on and lived. People love them so much. Now, these people that have grown up and are the ones that are directing and writing movies are throwing nods to us actresses. For instance, Rob Zombie with *The Devil's Rejects*. Rob put out a call for notably 1970s actors, when he was looking for cameos for the movie. When I went in, I brought a picture of me with my red baseball cap from *Carrie* and I signed it, "Dear Rob, I'm ready to scream for you again." And he hired me. I was in *Jawbreaker* because Darren Stein, the director-writer, who was like twenty-six at the time, wanted me and William Katt to play the parents. He thought it was such a cool thing because he loved us both in *Carrie*.

MATT: Speaking of *The Devil's Rejects*, what was that like for you?

P.J.: That was good. I only had that one scene. I was coming out of the store with my little son and I get

A recent headshot of P.J.

carjacked by Sid Haig's character, Captain Spaulding. It's very funny. It's a cool scene, and he punches me out, but he doesn't kill me, so I could be in a sequel.

MATT: What is the most common thing that people say to you when they meet you?

P.J.: The first thing is, "Oh, my god, I can't believe it's you!" And second is, "Oh, my god, *Halloween* is my favorite, you have no idea!" We are talking about people that could be sixteen years old, or they could be sixty years old. It's every age. People even push their little kids over to my table at autograph conventions. They say, "Little boy here has seen *Halloween* three times." And I say to the kid, "You have?" And they say, "You're the one who has the boyfriend." And it's like "Oh. You have." I am always surprised that parents let kids watch it. It shows you that the movie is really more about the fear of the unknown and the chills and thrills. Not the blood and the gore. Who wants to look at blood and gore? It's like a butcher shop. But actually feeling something pulls more on that raw emotion that gets you more scared than just a visual disgusting moment.

MATT: Couldn't have said it better myself. Thank you so much for taking the time out to talk to me, P. J.

P.J.: You're welcome. Thank you. I hope you can get it all down and make a good chapter.

MATT: Totally.

Chapter Fifteen:
ADRIENNE BARBEAU

Of all the actresses I have talked to for this book, none have had more labels than Adrienne Barbeau. She has been called a "Sex Symbol" and an "Action Heroine" for her roles on the silver screen. Her groundbreaking role on the television series *Maude* put her in the forefront of the 1970s women's movement and, most importantly for purposes of this book, a beloved "Scream Queen." She has worked for some of the greatest contemporaries in the horror genre: George A. Romero, Stephen King, Wes Craven, and her former husband, John Carpenter. Her many film roles include *Swamp Thing, Creepshow, The Fog,* and *Escape from New York,* among others. In recent years, she has added horror writer and soap-opera star to her ever-growing list of titles. Here is our interview done on the morning of September 6, 2009.

MATT:	With the recent passing of Beatrice Arthur a couple of months ago, I wanted to start out by talking about your work on *Maude* with her. What are some of your fondest memories of Bea?
ADRIENNE:	She was fantastic to work with. I think the thing that stands out to me most, when I think about Bea, is something that I took for granted at the time we were working together. I had never done a television show, and so I didn't have anything to compare it to. It wasn't until I did other guest-starring roles on other shows that I realized how incredibly professional she was and how incredibly

giving she was. I just sort of took it for granted. I thought everybody was that way, but they're not and Bea was. She was the first person in the rehearsal hall in the morning and the last person to leave. What I remember specifically is, when the cast would read the script that we were going to be shooting two weeks later, we would read it two weeks early, so that the writers could see if there were any problems, see if anything needed to be punched up a bit. And Bea was always the first to say, "I think this joke might be funnier if Conrad were saying it or Adrienne." It was all about the work and making the work the best it could be. She was just down to earth and caring about what we were doing.

MATT: Did you guys keep in touch after the series?

ADRIENNE: We did. I didn't see her very often. I don't know how well you know Los Angeles, but she lived in Mandeville Canyon and I live in Studio City. We might as well be living in two separate states. I rarely got out there. She came to visit after my twins were born. The last time I saw her, we were in New York together. The first season of *Maude* had come out on DVD, and so we did a bunch of press together. It was as though I had been with her the day before. She was just a great lady, she was a mom, and a dog lover, and those are the things I think about when I think about Bea. She loved her kids and she loved her dogs and she loved her work. Maybe she loved her success and her celebrity, but that wasn't why she did it. She was a brilliant comedienne.

MATT: How did you get involved with *Maude*?

ADRIENNE: If you read my book, *There Are Worse Things I Could Do*, that will tell you more specifically.

MATT: Can you give us the Reader's Digest version?

ADRIENNE: (Laughs). Yes. I was nominated for a Tony Award for playing Rizzo in *Grease* on Broadway. Norman Lear's casting people either came to see the show, or they heard about it, and they called me in for an interview with Norman. The role had already been cast, when they did the episode on *All in the Family* with Maude's character, but they were replacing that actress. She was a wonderful actress, but they felt, I think, that her comedic delivery was too much like Bea's. They wanted someone who had a bit of a different quality, and I also think the actress didn't want to relocate to Los Angeles. So, I went in to meet Norman, and based on our meeting, he felt that I looked too young. And so, that was the end of it. I figured, *Back to work, Adrienne.* About a month later, my agent showed up at the theatre and told me they wanted to see me in Los Angeles on Monday for an audition. Had it not been for the grace of the producers of *Grease*, Ken Waissman and Maxine Fox, who let me go to L.A., I never would have gotten the job.

MATT: The show dealt with a lot of taboo subjects that weren't talked about a lot on TV. Do you see anything on TV today that resembles that show for teenage girls?

ADRIENNE: I don't see anything on TV that resembles *Maude* in the way we dealt with issues of the time, and the classiness in which we dealt with issues, and in the entertaining aspects of the show. We were hitting people over the heads. I see things on cable that deal with some of the issues, but dealing with them in a much more graphic way. I don't watch much half-hour sitcoms. I don't watch any! So, I don't see any comedy that's dealing with social issues in the way that we did. They are much more explicit. Maybe more on the nose even.

MATT: Do you remember how the show was received when it first aired? It was ahead of its time and dealt with many social issues.

ADRIENNE: There were a lot of people who just hated Bea's character. They were probably threatened by her. She was too strong for some, too ballsy, and too tall (laughs). Of course, a lot of people found the show much too controversial. There were a lot of conservatives out there who hated the show and didn't want to see the topics we were dealing with on television at all. I mean, when the abortion episode aired, we had stations all over the country that refused to air the show.

MATT: Do you remember why the series was taken off the air?

ADRIENNE: Bea was tired. She wanted a break. I think she also wanted to go out while we were still in the Top 20. She probably thought six years was enough. She didn't want it to get to the point where the scripts were no longer good.

MATT: Not long after *Maude*, you met and soon married John Carpenter. Could you tell me how you guys met?

ADRIENNE: I met John when I auditioned for him. It was an interview, basically. He called me in for a television movie he was casting called *Someone's Watching Me*. I think he had seen my work on *Maude* and was attracted to the type of character I played. It was the type of character he liked to write. So, he called me in to offer me the job in *Someone's Watching Me.* We got to know each other on the set.

MATT: Was there an instant connection between the two of you?

ADRIENNE: I think so (laughs). I mean, I walked in and I thought, *Oh God, this is a nice looking guy.* I was very attracted to his talent and his expertise. He is a wonderful director. I would work with John in every film if I could. I loved working with him as a director. I trusted him completely.

MATT: Is it true that up until you met John, you had never watched a horror movie?

ADRIENNE: Yeah! I still haven't. Well, I've seen *Halloween* (laughing).

MATT: In your book, you said it was under duress?

ADRIENNE: Well, I didn't know going into it. I was under duress as I started watching it! I went to see it looking forward to seeing the film this guy that I'm engaged to had made. I don't remember ever seeing a horror film before that, and I certainly wasn't prepared. To this day, it's the scariest thing I have ever seen. I suppose other things have come out since, but I haven't seen them.

MATT: That being said, what did you think about your first feature film being a horror movie?

ADRIENNE: You know, when he first gave it to me, I never thought in terms of, *Oh, it's a horror movie*, or *It's this*, or *It's that.* I do remember when he first gave it to me to read, I was very involved in the woman's movement of that time. I remember thinking to myself, *He has all this talent. Why doesn't he write something that's going to change the world, like The China Syndrome?* I wanted him to make a movie with a message, and that's not John at all. And you know what? He probably did change the world with *The Fog*. It has had such a long life, and I still have people come up to me all the time saying, "I watch that movie once a month." I think he just changed it in a different way.

MATT: How was it working with your new husband on your first feature film?

ADRIENNE: We started out attempting to be so professional that we didn't even speak to each other. We stayed in separate rooms one night, and we wanted the rest of the cast to know that I wasn't going to get any preferential treatment because we were married (laughing). About halfway through the first day, John came up to me and said, "I'm not having any fun. I don't like this." I said, "Oh, forget it. Let's go back to being a husband and wife and having a good time."

MATT: Did you shoot in a real lighthouse?

ADRIENNE: The exteriors were shot in the Point Reyes National Seashore lighthouse. When it got too windy, we were shut down by the National Parks Department, or State Parks Department, whichever. If the wind got over a certain amount of knots an hour—I don't know how many—we weren't allowed to shoot on the property because it was too dangerous. There were a couple of days where we lost some filming time. The interiors were shot on a set in L.A.

Adrienne in a scene from *The Fog*.

MATT: Didn't you shoot one particular scene in reverse? I found that to be a fascinating bit of moviemaking. Could you share that with me?

ADRIENNE: Yes. This was before the days of CGI (Computer-Generated Imagery). They had to work with the fog, and the only way they could work with the fog, which was basically some kind of oil and coarsen mixture, I don't know, we just called it "Fog Juice." It was this oily stuff that smelled bad and got all over your body. It was horrible. The only way they could work with it was with fans, where they could blow it away. They couldn't suck it out. John came to me and said, "The only thing we can do is get the fog on you. We can't get the fog off of you, so we are going to have to shoot this in reverse, where it starts with the fog off of you and you are playing the end of the scene." In other words, the scene was: I am being threatened, I'm being chased, I'm terrified, I'm running away. Suddenly, the ghost disappears. I'm completely confused and bemused and then relieved because I am safe. We had to play it in reverse, we had to play it with no fog around me, feeling safe and relieved, and then bemused, and then covered in fog, and terrified! John said, "We will shoot in a reverse sequence and then do something in the processing where they printed the film backwards." Something like that. This is not my area of expertise. He said, "The only thing you have to be careful of is try not to blink or try not to blink fast, because if you blink fast when we reverse the film, it will look weird." That's all I know.

MATT: How did John feel about *The Fog* after he watched the first cut?

ADRIENNE: The first time he saw *The Fog*, he thought that he failed completely and should get out of the business. He didn't think it worked. He went back and he filmed some more scenes. The scene where Nancy is in her home and the chair scoots across the room was added. The scene in the mini mart, where the boys are sweeping up, and suddenly, all the lights start going off and on, and a couple of other scenes were added. Those were all shot after he completed his first pass, and they worked.

MATT: Do you have any favorite memories thirty years later?

ADRIENNE: I have wonderful memories of *The Fog*. I loved working in Inverness, California. John and I ended up buying a house there because we loved the area so much. I think the location is almost as much a character in *The Fog* as the characters are. I love the character of Stevie Wayne. I loved her philosophy of life. She knew she needed to stay there and save the town if she could by warning them about *The Fog.* I loved her strength and heroism. I am very proud of the movie.

MATT: Does its longevity surprise you at all?

ADRIENNE: No. It doesn't. It's sort of a timeless film and it's proven itself to be that.

MATT: You also worked with John in the hit film, *Escape from New York.* Had he written the role of Maggie for you? Did you have anything to do with her development, since I assume you were with John when he was developing the movie?

ADRIENNE: John did write Maggie with me in mind, but I had nothing to do with her development. Except that it was my idea to boil a turkey bone and use it for a hair clip. I felt it had to be something available inside the prison, although now, for the life of me, I don't remember how I justified having turkeys in Manhattan—maybe they were in the freezer section of Gristede's (a small chain of supermarkets based in New York City) before the government took over.

MATT: Is it true the studio originally did not want Kurt Russell for the role of Snake? Whom did they want?

ADRIENNE: The studio didn't believe Kurt could be an action hero. They were pushing for Tommy Lee Jones. Charles Bronson had expressed interest in playing the part. John just held out for Kurt; he wouldn't agree to anyone else.

MATT: What was it like working with Donald Pleasance?

Adrienne in *Escape from New York*.

ADRIENNE: Donald was a delight to work with. He was so
funny on the set, so witty, that there were moments
when I couldn't say my lines because he had me
laughing so hard. I still remember laughing hysterically
right before John was ready to call "action" and
begging him to wait a second so I could get myself
together. And Donald would just keep on talking
and making me laugh.

MATT: In your wonderful book, *There Are Worse Things I Could Do*, you write about the drawbridge scene at the end being one of your favorite scenes to film. Why is that?

ADRIENNE: The scene on the bridge is my favorite scene for Maggie because her entire being is exposed there. Her morality shows. There's no question in her mind about what to do to make it right for Brain when he's killed. She's not firing at The Duke out of anger. She's simply—I don't even want to use the word "avenge" because that carries with it too much negativity—she's just doing what she has to do to make it right.

MATT: Also in your book, you write about shooting Maggie dead in your home garage with John. Could you share that experience with me?

ADRIENNE: After John put the film together and screened it for the first time, there was some question in the minds of the audience about what had happened to Maggie. So, he decided we needed to see her dead. Filming in St. Louis was long past, but all we needed was a shot of me dead on the ground. I boiled another turkey bone, put on the costume and make-up, and parked my car on the street so we'd have space in our garage. Then, I laid down, they poured blood around my head, and John shot the shot.

MATT: After three projects with John, how would you reflect on those experiences with him as a husband/director?

ADRIENNE: I love working with John. We actually did four films together: I was the voice of the computer in *The Thing*. He's just the best. I trust him completely. You couldn't ask for a better director. His sets are a happy place to be!

MATT: You also worked with another beau of yours, Burt Reynolds, in the comedy *Cannonball Run*. Did you enjoy working on that film? It looked like a ton of fun.

ADRIENNE: I really didn't enjoy working on *Cannonball Run*, at least, not as much as fans of the film expect I should have. I loved meeting Roger Moore, and Dean (Martin), and Dom (Deluise) were both great fun to work with, but the whole thing was put together in sort of a slapdash manner and I wasn't terribly comfortable with it. Plus, we had a couple of tragic accidents on the set and that colored the whole experience for me. (Author's note: one such accident involved stuntwoman Heidi Von Beltz, who was left a paraplegic after crashing her car during a stunt.)

MATT: What was it like filming *Swamp Thing*? It looked really uncomfortable being out in the elements.

ADRIENNE: *Swamp Thing* was filmed in South Carolina. It was hot and muggy, and I spent most nights scratching chigger bites and checking my skin for ticks. We were constantly on the lookout for gators. The swamp was so polluted we had to plug our ears with antibacterial swabs before we went in the water and then wash off right away with disinfectant; and the stunt men's favorite pastime was finding snakes they could tease me with. But they were great guys, working in difficult surroundings, and they did a great job. It was a difficult shoot for all of us, Wes especially, because the film was so under-budgeted. He had to make daily compromises to get the work done. He made magic out of a nightmare situation.

Adrienne in a scene from *Swamp Thing*.

MATT: After *Swamp Thing*, you did *Creepshow*. Is it true
             you almost lost the role?

ADRIENNE: No, it's not true that I almost lost the role in
             Creepshow. I almost turned it down though. When
             I first read the script, not knowing the style George
             intended for it, it was so gross and bloody I didn't
             want to do it. I didn't know George's work at the
             time, but I did know Tom Atkins, who was a close

friend and who had already been cast in the movie. I called Tom to say I really didn't think I could do it, and he set me straight. He said George was going to shoot it like a comic book, and in my reading of it, I hadn't gotten any of the humor and style George intended. And, of course, I had John Carpenter telling me I was nuts to turn down an opportunity to work with George, the Master of Horror. So, I decided I didn't know what I was talking about, and took a chance on being in the film, and, of course, Billie turned out to be one of my all-time favorite characters. I still can't watch E. G. Marshall and the roaches, though.

MATT: When you travel the country doing horror conventions, what is the one thing you hear most from fans?

ADRIENNE: I guess I hear three things repeatedly from the fans I meet at horror conventions: "They never should have remade *The Fog*, I can't believe they cancelled *Carnivale*—it was the best show on television, and just call me Billie—everyone does."

MATT: In recent years, you starred on the brilliant HBO series, *Carnivale*. Did you enjoy going back into a television series after all those years?

ADRIENNE: I loved doing *Carnivale* more than almost any other job I've ever had. Well, *Fiddler on the Roof* on Broadway and *Grease* on Broadway were both fantastic jobs, too, but in terms of television, you couldn't ask for anything better than *Carnivale*. For all sorts of reasons: the words, the character, the cast, the writers, the location, even the lunch truck. And it was a great job for me as a mom. I still had time to be with my kids, get them to school, and help with homework.

MATT: I think I speak for millions when I say the show ended way too soon. As an actress, how did it make you feel saying goodbye to a show that was so loved by fans and critics alike?

ADRIENNE: I loved doing *Carnivale*—absolutely loved it. First of all, Ruthie was a once-in-a-lifetime role. How often does an actress over fifty get to play anything other than a judge, a nurse, or someone's mother? I was playing a snake dancer, for God's sake! She was a woman who was wise, sensual, and sexual, an Earth-mother, who saw dead people. It doesn't get much better than that. I loved the writers and producers and the cast. It was a joy to go to work every day. Even the caterers were great. Plus, having such a big cast gave me time off each week to spend with my kids. It was the ideal job, and I was incredibly proud of the work we all did.

MATT: What was the reason it was cancelled?

ADRIENNE: One of the hardest parts about appearing at the sci-fi/horror conventions is hearing so many fans express their disappointment that the show was cancelled. It was an expensive show to produce, and HBO didn't feel it garnered high enough ratings to merit the cost. I believe if we had stayed on the air for a third season, the ratings would have kept us there for a long time.

MATT: I agree. I think it was just finding its core audience when they pulled the plug. Recently, you have focused a lot on writing. What prompted you to write an autobiography?

ADRIENNE: I never set out to write an autobiography; it really was never my intention. I stumbled upon a writing class, which I began attending primarily because I'd lost my best friend to breast cancer and I thought it might be something to take my mind off the space in my life her passing had left. Well, I learned pretty quickly that if you're going to take a writing class, you need to write, or you won't fulfill your homework assignments. So, I started writing about some of the experiences I'd had, starting with my career as a teenager alone in New York City working for the mob, landing on Broadway, dating Burt Reynolds, all things I took for granted, but was vaguely aware that they might be interesting to people who hadn't lived them. Things like starring in a horror film in Moscow with a bunch of rats, the long snout, and long-tailed kind. After I wrote four or five of these short pieces, my teacher suggested I show them to a literary agent, and the next thing I knew, I had a contract to write a memoir. No one was more surprised than I was.

MATT: Your biography ended with you about to tackle the role of Judy Garland in an Off-Broadway play your husband, Billy Van Zandt, wrote and produced. How did the show go?

ADRIENNE: *The Property Known As Garland* was a huge success with the audiences—standing ovations every night. Unfortunately, the New York critics didn't all love it, so we never moved it from Off-Broadway to another venue. But I have people from all over the country tell me they saw it and loved it, and that's always nice to hear.

MATT: You also wrote a horror novel titled *Vampryes of Hollywood.* Where did the inspiration come from?

ADRIENNE: *Vampyres of Hollywood* came out of a conversation with an Irish author, Michael Scott, who was

Adrienne Barbeau today.
PHOTO COURTESY OF ADRIENNE BARBEAU.

visiting my writing teacher. Michael had read *There Are Worse Things I Could Do*, and he suggested I should write a horror novel for all the genre fans out there who love to watch *The Fog* and *Creepshow* and all my other horror films. When I expressed some anxiety about writing fiction, he offered to collaborate with me, and so we did. We sold two books in the series, and I ended up writing the second one by myself. It will be published in 2010.

MATT: Lastly, What projects are you currently working on? Isn't there another novel on the way?

ADRIENNE: I've got several films "in the can." Two of them are making the festival circuit right now and winning some nice awards, and I just finished guest-starring in a handful of television shows. I'm taking a break from writing so I can spend my weekends at my boys' soccer tournaments, but I'll probably get back to it in the spring. And I'm back in school, learning Japanese so I can hold my own in a conversation when I visit my older son, who's living in Tokyo. In the meantime, when an acting job comes along that appeals to me, I'm there. I never know what I'll be doing next, but I always know it never feels like work.

MATT: Thank you a million times over, Adrienne.

Conclusion

After reading this book, I hope you walk away with something. After doing the interview with Marilyn Burns and watching *The Texas Chainsaw Massacre*, it heightened the experience for me. When I saw Marilyn get cut, I squirmed in my seat, more so than I had always done in the past. I recommend watching some of the horror movies discussed in this book after reading the interviews with their respective stars. Having some insight into their thought processes and behind-the-scenes information gives you a bit more to experience.

I never imagined when setting out to do this book the wealth of information it would contain. Not to mention the fascinating stories of each included actress. I think you will agree with me in applauding each of the actresses, for they are the ladies who helped pave the way for future generations of "Scream Queens." One can only hope that whatever the future holds in terms of horror movies, the ladies in the films will live up to the challenges and the time-honored tradition of being a "Scream Queen."

About the Author

Matt Beckoff has contributed to *Classic Images* magazine, as well as *Films of the Golden Age* magazine. He hosts a weekly radio broadcast titled *The Beckoff Show*. He lives in New Jersey.

He can be reached at

PO Box 363
Elmwood Park, NJ 07407